disciple-making
teachers

by josh hunt
with
dr. larry mays

disciple-making
teachers

by josh hunt with
dr. larry mays

Special thanks to Mike Stone and Lou Cowden for helpful editorial comments.

Credits

Editor: Bob Buller

Quality Control Editor: Paul Woods

Chief Creative Officer: Joani Schultz

Copy Editor: Helen Turnbull

Art Director: Ray Tollison

Cover Art Director: Paul Povolni

Computer Graphic Artist: Joyce Douglas

Cover Designer: Rebecca Parrott

Production Manager: DeAnne Lear

Library of Congress Cataloging-in-Publication Data

Hunt, Josh.

    Disciple-making teachers / by Josh Hunt with Larry Mays.

Contents

Introduction 5

  The Big Picture. 5

  The Importance of Good Teaching 6

  What Is Good Teaching? .8

  What's the Point?. 10

Section One: 12

  What Is a Disciple?. 13

    Disciplined 15

    Intimate Friendships 20

    Self-Esteem 22

    Corporate Worship 27

    Intimate Family Life. 29

    Passion for God. 33

    Lay Ministry. 36

    Evangelistic Interest 40

    Sacrificial Giving 43

Section Two: 47

  Barriers to Learning. 48

  The Learning Process. 53

Section Three: 66

  Asking Good Questions. 67

  The Repeated Phrase. 83

Stuff You Can Touch and Feel 85

Video 87

Review, Review, Review 89

Giving Everyone a Chance to Talk 93

Prayer in the Classroom 95

Reading Your Students 98

When Not to Teach 101

Laughter 105

Section Four: 110

Whole-Brained Preparation 111

We Teach So Little Because We Try to Teach
     So Much 114

Reading Books 116

Closing Thoughts 120
     I Love It! 121

The Heart of a Teacher 122

Introduction
The Big Picture

The Importance of Good Teaching

What a difference good teaching makes! In my last book, You Can Double Your Class in Two Years or Less (Group Publishing, 1997), I emphasized all the things you can do to make people want to become a part of your class or small group. I suggested that you invite every member and every visitor to every fellowship every month, that you give Friday nights to Jesus, that you invite group members and group prospects to a time of informal hospitality in your home, and that you recruit a team of people to help you in this work.

These things are important, but none is as important as "teaching a halfway decent lesson each and every week." I have seen teachers who did very little outreach but grew their classes marvelously on the sheer power of their teaching. On the other hand, as someone in Oklahoma remarked, "Good visitation cannot overcome bad teaching." People come to where the food is. Word of mouth can grow a class if the teacher consistently delivers the goods.

Don't hear this as a recanting of the things I said in my earlier book. It isn't. I still believe we can reach America with the gospel through groups that are doubling (reproducing) every two years or less. I still believe that most people who are opposed to the gospel are not opposed to love. I still believe that if we will love people they will come to love our Lord.

However, I have an increasing conviction regarding the vital role of teaching. Teachers who teach well never lack for an audience. Teachers who teach well change lives. Teachers who teach well make disciples.

> Teachers who teach well never lack for an audience. Teachers who teach well change lives. Teachers who teach well make disciples.

Bill Hybels of Willow Creek Community Church, for example, has led the way with the seeker-driven paradigm, the seven-step strategy, networking, and various other innovative ministry strategies. But when I hear Bill Hybels preach his average weekend seeker message or midweek New Community message, I think to myself, "Willow Creek's strategy could be dead wrong, and he would still fill the auditorium."

You see, it's really not about networking or the seven-step strategy or all the rest of these excellent approaches. It is about the fact that Bill Hybels puts it together on stage. When he talks, people listen. I just smile when I hear that Midwestern accent because I know he will probably deliver another great message.

It's the same with Rick Warren, senior pastor of Saddleback Valley Community Church. He has clearly articulated his ideas about the purpose-driven church.[1] He can identify differences between his approach and Willow Creek's strategy (though to the casual observer the two sound rather similar). He can explain the difference between form and function well enough that I know what can be applied directly and what I must adapt. But when I hear one of his sermons, I think, "What a difference good teaching makes! People would come to hear him even if he had no strategy at all."

That's why I've come to believe that the number one variable in predicting the growth (or nongrowth) of a church is not its program or philosophy of ministry. It is not the pastor's theology or the church's location. The single most important factor is the pastor's ability to teach. If the pastor preaches well, growth is easy, almost assured. If, on the other hand, the pastor doesn't preach well, no amount of drama, contemporary music, seeker-sensitive services, or other outreach strategies is really going to help. In the same way, the single most important variable in predicting the growth of a Sunday school class or a small group is the teaching ability of the teacher.

Now, if your small group or Sunday school class is not growing rapidly, you could respond in several ways. You could become depressed that you are the reason for your group's lack of growth. You might even reject the notion that the communication skill of the leader has more to do with the growth of any organization than anything else and blame the lack of growth on some other factor. Or you could optimistically see that communication is something you control. If your group's growth has more to do with your ability to teach than any other factor, this is good news because it is the one thing over which you have the most control.

The best thing is to have great teaching and great strategies, and there is no reason you cannot have both. Outreach strategies can help you double your class in two years or less, assuming that someone has something to say when people show up for class. But if someone is not doing a reasonably good job teaching, no amount of inviting, parties, or ice cream will help.

Perhaps a grid will help explain what I mean.

1. Poor teaching/Poor group life	2. Good teaching/ Poor group life
3. Poor teaching/ Good group life	4. Good teaching/ Good group life

Several things should be obvious. Groups in quadrant 1 have very little chance of growing. Yet we all have some groups like this in our churches. They linger on somehow, sometimes for years, but only due to the grace of God. Quadrant 4 is optimal. The combination of an active group life that reaches out to and loves others with sizzling, mind-stretching, spiritually challenging teaching—that is what produces real growth.

But what about quadrants 2 and 3? Which is better? Which type of group has a better chance of growing? Which has a better chance of creating disciples? I would bet on quadrant 2 every time. I would choose good teaching over good group life because good teaching will generally produce far better results than good group life ever can on its own.

Of course, I don't like having to make that choice. I still like quadrant 4 groups best. Jesus spoke of seed falling on good soil and producing thirty, sixty, or a hundred times what was sown (Mark 4:20). Groups with good teaching and good group life are like good soil that produces results.

The differences really are staggering. I encourage you to evaluate the classes in your church to see which are growing and which are not. I did such a study once and discovered that 90 percent of the church's growth was coming out of one class. One class!

What was going on in that class? Good teaching *and* good group life. What if every group in your church had good teaching and good group life? What if just half the groups did? What if half the groups in half the churches in America were characterized by strong group life and strong teaching? What if!

You do not have to teach as well as Chuck Swindoll or Bill Hybels. Halfway decent teaching can grow a class. But how much better a class will be when teaching is excellent, when the teacher consistently prepares and delivers lessons that create disciples. The purpose of this book is to help you become that kind of teacher.

What Is Good Teaching?

This book is about becoming a better teacher, so maybe we should define our terms. Just what is "good teaching"?

Some define good teaching as *deep* teaching. (I'm still waiting for someone to tell me that one of my lessons was deep.) People often use the word "deep" to describe teaching that is hard to understand. That is not good teaching. It is muddy teaching.

For some, good teaching is equated with a certain methodology. Lots of people, for example, are critical of lecture, but I have heard some lectures that would certainly qualify as good teaching. For me, there is nothing better than an engaging, life-challenging lecture. Most lectures, however, aren't that good. So group discussion has become far more popular. Involvement. Participation. Sharing. Unfortunately, you can do all of that and still be lousy at teaching.

Variety is one textbook answer. I even taught this one myself: "Use any method except the one you used last week." Variety, that's what makes you effective, isn't it? Yes…unless you are moving from one ineffective method to the next. In addition, I have heard people do pretty much the same thing every week and still be great.

So what is great teaching? Simply put, great teaching is teaching that creates great people. Where disciples of Jesus are being developed, great teaching is taking place. Jesus' teaching was great, not because his stories were interesting (which they were), but because his disciples turned the world upside down. When the people in our small groups and classes turn their worlds upside down, we have done a reasonably good job of teaching. Jesus told us to make disciples, not merely to make converts (Matthew 28:19-20). The objective of Christian teaching is to produce mature disciples of Jesus Christ.

Teaching is not about methods. It is about results, about changed lives. We are out to create people who enjoy God and get along with others. Paul, by his own admission, wasn't eloquent (1 Corinthi-ans 2:4), but he changed lives. He reminds the Co-rinthians, "You show that you are a letter from Christ, the result of our ministry, written not with ink but with the Spirit of the living God, not on tablets of stone but on tablets of human hearts" (2 Corinthians 3:3). So I ask: Who can you point to and say, "This person is living the disciple's life because of my teaching ministry"? Teaching that makes disciples is good teaching. Anything less is simply not enough.

> Teaching is not about methods. It is about results, about changed lives.

If we cannot point to men and women, boys and girls who love God and others, we have failed. Gathering a large crowd—even doubling our classes!—doesn't make us successful. Teaching lessons that everyone compliments for their insight and relevance doesn't make us great teachers. Both of these miss the point of good teaching. The point is to change lives, to help people live differently on Monday morning. Teaching that produces disciples is good teaching.

What's the Point?

Soon after he began teaching, my friend Ken Woods asked me, "How much time should I spend preparing to teach my lesson?" My answer was on target, as far as it went: "That isn't really the point, Ken. The point is not what you do at home—it's what you do in class. We all have busy schedules, so if you can prepare a lesson that will be a "10" in two hours, don't spend four hours preparing it." There is no virtue in spending unnecessary time preparing a particular lesson. All things being equal, the less time we spend the better.

That was my answer to Ken, but it didn't go nearly far enough. The point is not what happens in the teacher's home in preparation or what happens with the teacher in class in presentation. The point is what happens with the learner. The test of teaching is never what the teacher does; it is what the class members learn.

This is why videos can supplement your lessons: If a thirty-minute video by Chuck Swindoll says it better than you ever could, why not use it? If the student learns, the teacher has taught. (See pages 88-89 for more on using videos in class.) I have heard teachers argue, "I just don't feel fulfilled as a teacher if all I do is punch the play button on a video recorder." But, you see, the class does not exist so that the teacher can feel fulfilled. The teacher exists so that the class will learn. Who cares that the teacher did not have to spend time preparing the lecture?

Teaching is not about certain gestures or questions or stories or activities. Teaching is not about the teacher at all. Teaching is about people learning. If a video will, in fact, help people learn better than any other method, then it is the method to use, even if it doesn't make the teacher feel important or fulfilled. Teaching is not about making the teacher feel important. It is about serving a group by leading them to learn.

After several years of meditating on this, I realized a deeper insight: The real point is not even what happens with the learner in class. Teaching is not about people feeling moved in class; it is about people moving when they get out of class. The point is not how high people jump, but how straight they walk when they get down. What happens in class matters, but not as much as what happens in people's homes, workplaces, lives, and relationships. The point is not that the students feel entertained or interested or stimulated or whatever. The point is—will they live differently Monday morning?

Let me illustrate this graphically.

> Teaching is not about people feeling moved in class; it is about people moving when they get out of class.

This is what disciple-making teaching is all about. It is about

	Outside of Class	In Class
Teacher	Preparation	Presentation
Learner	Lifestyles	Learning

results. Results lived out in lives of people every day. Results like people who love their spouses and know how to meet their needs. Results like people who love God with all their heart, soul, mind, and strength. Results like people effectively ministering in the areas of their giftedness and loving it.

What is the point? Not how long I prepare. Not what I do in class or what happens with learners in class. The point is what happens in the lives of class members at home, in the workplace, and at play as a result of what has happened in class. The point is people's lives Monday morning.

In order to produce the desired results in people's lives, the right thing must be happening with them in class. It's unlikely that people who are bored in class will be different when they wake up Monday morning. To produce change in people's lives, the teacher has to do the right things in class. And in order for the teacher to do the right things in class, he or she must prepare the right way. That is what this book is about: solid preparation that produces effective presentation that produces life-changing moments for people in class that produce disciples of Jesus on Monday morning.

In fact, this book is organized around these four quadrants, and we will examine each one in detail: lifestyle, learning, presentation, and preparation. And since the point is how people live on Monday morning and every day of their lives, we will begin with that end in mind, with the lifestyle of a disciple of Jesus.

otes

[1] Rick Warren, *The Purpose-Driven Church*. Grand Rapids, MI: Zondervan, 1995.

Section One:
The Learner Outside of Class

	Outside of Class	In Class
Teacher	Preparation	Presentation
Learner	Lifestyles	Learning

What Is a Disciple?

One of the oddest things about church life is that we have no good way of measuring how well we are doing what Jesus told us to do. It's not as though we don't know how to count or are unwilling to count. We count almost everything. My denomination, for example, can cite reams of statistics down to children's choir attendance and other such details. But we have no good way of measuring the main task with which Jesus left us: to make disciples (Matthew 18:19-20).

We have no good way of measuring how well we are doing what Jesus told us to do.

Attendance figures are not an accurate reflection of how many disciples are in our group. Some of those who attend are, in fact, disciples, while others are not yet believers. In addition, even the best of disciples don't show up for every single class or small group. Although we might describe them as living the disciple's life, they only show up on attendance rolls when they actually come. Attendance merely measures how many bodies show up.

This is why we need disciple-making teachers. Teachers can draw close enough to people to know whether they are living the disciple's life. Disciple-making teachers can influence people to make the next step in the learning and maturing process. Teachers can get close enough to help people become disciples of Jesus Christ.

Fundamentally, the biblical word for "disciple" means learner or student. Of course, few people aspire to be lifelong students. Many become students for a short while, but generally as a means to an end. They usually have some larger goal in mind. But Jesus called us to be permanently in the classroom. The word "disciple" does not imply a static state. It implies someone who is growing, improving, reaching, stretching.

The word "disciple" also means follower. In Jesus' day it was customary for a teacher to travel around while his students literally followed him. They would ask questions and dialogue as they walked along with him. Thus, a disciple was one who followed Christ, who walked in his ways and sought to imitate him.

Today the word "disciple" is used in a wide variety of ways with reference to everything from evangelism to Scripture memory. It is even used in secular literature, as it was in Jesus' day. Because of this, we need to carefully define the kind of person we are trying to create. We need to define "disciple" in terms of the etymology of the Greek word *and* in terms of the entire gospel message. We also need to define "disciple" in a culturally relevant way that makes sense in the place and time God has called us to serve.

I encourage you to work out your own definition of "disciple." Ask yourself what it means to be a disciple of Jesus today and every day. What are the minimum requirements of discipleship? If possible, try to devise some linguistic or visual means of communicating these in a memorable way.

For example, Dawson Trotman, founder of the Navigators, did this with the wheel illustration.[1] Christ was at the center of the wheel. Branching out from him were four spokes depicting the Word (the foundational spoke), prayer, witnessing, and fellowship. The words "The Obedient Christian" were written around the rim. When I first saw Trotman's illustration, I thought that it defined discipleship in a helpful way. However, at least one thing seems to be missing: the articulation of an emphasis on family life. These days, we need to spell this out. So I looked for other definitions of discipleship.

Eventually I came across Bill Hybels's definition of discipleship.[2] He defines discipleship in terms of five G's:

Grace. A disciple has experienced grace (salvation) and is walking in grace.

Growth. A disciple is growing in his or her relationship with Christ.

Group. A disciple is vitally involved in some sort of Christian group.

Gifts. A disciple knows what his or her spiritual gifts are and uses them in ministry.

Good Stewardship. A disciple gives his or her time, talents, and resources to kingdom causes.

Hybels's list also provided useful insight into what it means to be a disciple. However, it didn't seem to be detailed enough. I believed that we need to clearly articulate that part of discipleship that relates to people's everyday lives. With the help of my friend, Lance Witt, I developed a rough definition, an acrostic based on the word DISCIPLES. I taught this at various seminars and then asked for feedback. I asked if there were anything unnecessary in our list or if we had left out any issues essential to a biblical definition of discipleship. In time, with the help of numerous people, I decided on the version that I would like to place before you. I am confident that if we can create people who are characterized by these nine traits, we will be fairly close to the biblical model of making disciples. So here are the nine traits I feel are critical to being a disciple of Jesus:

D   A disciple is **disciplined** in his or her daily life.

I A disciple enjoys **intimate friendships** with others.
S A disciple's **self-esteem** reflects God's view of him or her.
C A disciple is involved in **corporate worship**.
I A disciple experiences an **intimate family life**.
P A disciple feels true and compelling **passion for God**.
L A disciple is involved in some sort of **lay ministry**.
E A disciple has an **evangelistic interest**.
S A disciple is committed to **sacrificial giving**.

A fascinating exercise for any church, class, or small group is to work through the same process together, to define what you are trying to create through your ministry. It doesn't matter if your list is different from this one. What matters is that you have a clearly defined goal regarding the kind of people you are trying to develop. One thing is certain: If you don't know what you are trying to achieve, it is unlikely that you will reach your goals.

A tool such as the DISCIPLES acrostic does provide one way to measure our obedience to the Great Commission. I recently asked a group of Sunday school teachers how many of the people who attend their classes are doing reasonably well in each of these nine areas. "How many are involved in some kind of ministry? How many have reasonably good marriages?" In the opinion of these teachers, about 25 percent of their class members are giving the disciple's life the old college try. Surely we can do better than that. Perhaps it is time to start tracking discipleship instead of simply counting how many people attend each week. Maybe we need to ask people to "grade" themselves on how well they are living the disciple's life.

In order to do this, however, we need to clearly understand what we are aiming for. So in the pages that follow, we will explore each of these nine characteristics in greater detail.

Disciplined

Imagine, if you will, a row of nine dominoes, all standing on end. Your goal is to knock all nine down, but you can only touch one. Which one do you push? The one on the end, right? In my opinion, "disciplined in daily life" is much like an "end" domino. If this trait falls, all the others will probably topple over as well.

Discipline often carries negative connotations, but when I speak of discipline, I have in mind primarily the discipline (or habit) of spending time every day praying to God and meditating on his Word. If we can teach people to spend time alone with God nearly every day, we have some hope of developing in them the other eight traits of a disciple. But if we are unable to help people develop this habit, it is unlikely that we will ever make biblical disciples.

Discipline is perhaps the most misunderstood aspect of what it means to be a disciple. People often use the word to refer to "doing what I ought to do instead of what I want to do" or "doing what I should do, not what I really like doing." But we are not trying to create people who read their Bible and pray even though they do not feel like it (though that may be an intermediate step). Our ultimate goal is to create people who *feel* like reading their Bible and praying. Disciple-making teachers seek to create people who pray whenever they want to...and want to quite regularly.

Biblical discipleship is all about the heart, about motives. It is about creating people of passion and desire. It is not about law and "should" and "ought to." At times we must do one thing when we want to do another—that is responsibility. But that is not the heart and soul of Christian discipleship. That is the stuff of law, the stuff of the Old Covenant, the stuff of the Pharisees.

Disciple-making teachers do not merely present rules. They are fundamentally after a change of people's hearts. They are out to create people who, as Augustine explained, love God, love others, and do whatever they want. Disciple-making teachers are out to create people who pray because they want to, who read the Bible when they feel like it and feel like it often, who serve as much as they want to and want to quite a bit. Disciple-making teachers seek to create people who do all of this, not out of law or obligation, but out of their heart's desire.

> disciple-making teachers seek to create people who pray whenever they want to...and want to quite regularly.

So how do you create people like this? How do you create people who want to pray, read their Bibles, serve, give, and love? One thing is certain. Guilt and law don't work. Two thousand years of Old Testament history prove that beyond any doubt. Still, it seems we haven't gotten the message. We think we can get people to do better by telling them what they should do and what they shouldn't do. The Bible has a word for this.

Law.

Trust me, it doesn't work. Giving people the notion that God will love them more if they read their Bibles is wrong, yet it happens all the time. Whether teachers say it explicitly or only allow people to jump to their own conclusions, it happens, and it is wrong. We should never use God's love as a threat.

This is not a minor matter. It touches at the heart of the gospel. The gospel is about grace, about a God who loves us completely no matter what. Sometimes we find it too easy to preach a "grace-and" gospel—a little bit of grace *and* a little bit of law. But the gospel is all grace, nothing less and nothing more.

Even if we don't preach a "grace-and" gospel, people may hear one anyway. The "grace-alone" gospel of the Bible is radical in its concept of salvation and in its concept of discipleship. Both are all about grace. Left to themselves, people often assume a grace-and gospel. So we must constantly and vigilantly teach otherwise.

We must teach the biblical view that people become slaves to sin (Romans 7:7-25). Slaves. If we understood and believed these verses, we would take more seriously the addicts when they say that they can't stop. They want to change, but they can't. I am not referring merely to alcohol, drugs, or other common addictions. All sin is addictive, which means that people cannot stop. They are powerless to stop.

If we truly understand this, we will stop giving platitudes about how people who are sinning simply need to quit. Telling people they are sinning and need to quit simply will not work.

Pressuring people to follow specific Bible-reading or spiritual-discipline programs won't produce long-term change, either. Specific programs may help for a while, but they are crutches. There's nothing wrong with crutches when we need them, but we shouldn't confuse walking with crutches with real walking.

For example, challenging people to read one chapter of Proverbs each day for a month or to read through the entire Bible in a year may be a useful way to help them develop the habit of reading their Bibles regularly. But we must remember that these programs are crutches. Our goal should be to help people fall in love with the Word, not with the crutches.

If we can't use law to bully people into being disciplined whether they feel like it or not, and we can't rely on programs for long-term change, how can we create people who are disciplined in their daily lives?

First, we need to put people in touch with their *deepest* desires. God's Word teaches that Christians are no longer slaves to sin because God has changed their "want-to." Philippians 2:13, for example, states that "God is at work within you, helping you want to obey him, and then helping you do what he wants" (The Living Bible). Eugene Peterson paraphrases verses 12-13 as follows: "Be energetic in your life of salvation, reverent and sensitive before God. That energy is God's energy, and energy deep within you, God himself willing and working at what will give him the most pleasure."

We need to regularly get people in touch with these God-given desires. Almost every week we should ask questions such as…

- If you could change one thing about your prayer life, what would it be?
- What personal characteristics do you most long to develop in your life?
- What is your greatest longing or desire with regard to the Bible?
- What would you like your relationship with your spouse to be like?

We also need to talk freely and honestly about our own desire to live the disciple's life. We need to say things such as…

- I want to know Jesus so well that I can really feel what life was like for him.
- I have such a hunger to understand, memorize, and apply these verses to my life.
- I want to grasp these truths so deeply that my life is totally changed.
- Playing with and imparting my values to my kids is more important than just about anything else.

In the long run, your example will do more to motivate people to develop discipline in their daily lives than anything else. We need to be able to say, as Paul did, "Follow my example, as I follow the example of Christ" (1 Corinthians 11:1). We need to tell stories of our own struggles and successes with personal discipline. We should also invite others to share their successes and struggles to develop a heart of discipline. One of the most motivating influences in life is the positive example of a friend. When people hear that someone else has succeeded at something, they begin to believe that they can as well. So teachers ought to regularly invite class members to share how the truth is working in their lives. Let the more mature be an example to those just starting down the path of discipleship.

Most of all, we need to cultivate an atmosphere of acceptance and grace. We must admit and accept that failure is part of the process. We need to represent God to each other by treating others as he does, with grace and truth. If we don't cultivate this atmosphere, people will not feel free to recognize and deal with lesser desires that are getting in the way of their souls' deepest desires. When, on the other hand, we treat people with acceptance and grace, we create for them a safe place where they can grow as disciples of Jesus.

This does not mean, of course, that we should not hold people accountable. Grace is not softness. It is not doing what you want to do and thinking that you are a disciple. We are out to produce disciples in the best sense of the word.

Creating disciples involves accountability. But please understand: Accountability is not law. Accountability is not pressuring people into doing what they don't want to do. Accountability is helping people keep *their* commitments. The key word is their.

Holding people accountable for what I think they should do is law. Helping them do what they decide to do is accountability. If someone agrees to hold me accountable, I decide what I want them to hold me accountable for and *how* I want to be held accountable.

> **a**ccountability is helping people keep *their* commitments.

How does this work out in a small group or class? Suppose our lesson is on reading God's Word. If I challenged the group to read a certain portion of Scripture every day, they might all get on board and even walk out of class thinking, "I'm going to do that." However, people being the way they are, it is unlikely that they will follow through on their "commitment." We all need accountability.

Rather, we should ask people, "How would you like to apply this lesson to your life, and how can we serve you by holding you accountable to your commitment?" Some may decide not to commit to anything at all, and we should accept and respect their decision. Others may make personal commitments but decline any sort of accountability. When that happens, we should let them try (even if we believe that they will fail). Accountability works only when people see and feel their need for it. Forcing commitments on people is little more than pharisaism.

Some will commit to read their Bible every day and ask us to hold them accountable for it. In those cases, we must make sure that we keep people accountable to do what they said they would do. I have seen accountability groups totally fail because they rewarded unkept commitments: "Did you read your Bible this week?" "No." "Well, don't feel bad—neither did I." We are to spur one another on to love and good works (Hebrews 10:24), but this kind of accountability only produces more and more failure. If people ask you to hold them accountable, do it. Periodically ask them how they are doing with their commitments. Help them develop the daily disciplines that characterize a disciple of Jesus.

You may want to provide general accountability times during the meeting and encourage private accountability on more personal issues. Too much open accountability will kill a group's outreach potential. You need to maintain a delicate balance. One way to strike this balance is by limiting in-class accountability to short-term, lesson-related issues and by initiating other opportunities for private accountability. For example, you might routinely encourage class members to check up on each other before or after class. You might also help people form same-sex pairs or trios in which they can talk regularly and frankly about their marriages, their relationship with God, parenting issues, and the like.

In all likelihood, you will be unable to hold everyone in your class or small group accountable for all that they commit to do. Simply remembering their commitments is a challenge in itself. But God has provided an answer to this dilemma. It is hidden in the two dozen or so of the New Testament's "one another" passages. According to the Bible, ministry does not come from the top-down; it extends from "one to another."

Ultimately, our ministry to the class should create ministry within the class. Our goal is to help class members minister to each other. This is what the body of Christ is all about: Christians helping each other develop discipline in their daily lives, people encouraging each other to become committed disciples of Christ. God designed the church to be a level organization where, as Francis Schaeffer said, there are "no little people,"[3] where people help each other develop the daily disciplines that characterize a disciple of Jesus.

These relationships form an integral part of becoming and being a disciple. "One another" relationships are the heart and soul of the New Testament church. In fact, they are so crucial that we will deal with them in some detail in the next discussion.

Intimate Friendships

I was chatting with my longtime friend Lance Witt the other day, when he asked, "You know what most people long for?" Lance posed the question because he wanted to answer it. I let him. "Most people long for the kind of friendships that we enjoyed in college." I think he's probably right.

The college Lance and I attended afforded the perfect opportunity for friendships to develop. Wayland University had, at that time, about five hundred resident students. Our freshman year, Lance and I happened to be next door neighbors. Bill Sloan, David Edwards, Rex Bell, and Andrew Large all lived close by. We would all walk to meals together, play cards together, and spend our evenings together talking about the issues of life. In a small school such as Wayland, everyone knew everyone else anyway, but the six of us developed a friendship that we will always treasure.

Friendships such as these are not as easy to develop in the adult world of kids and jobs and yards and bills. Still, they are just as important for adults as for anyone else. This means that what came naturally for the six of us at Wayland will need to be developed intentionally in the real world. We must work to form these kinds of friendships.

Our souls crave this kind of friendship. Our souls long to be close to someone else. It is part of being created in the image of God. The three persons of the Trinity are in relationship with each other, and since we are in God's image, we were made for relationships.

The Bible has a great deal to say about relationships. They form the basis of church life. In addition, love is to be the distinguishing mark of the people of God. Jesus taught that both Christians and non-Christians will know that we are his disciples if, and only if, we love one another (John 13:35).

Unfortunately, we need to rethink many of our ideas about love, relationships, and friendships. For example, many people teach that love is *nothing more* than a decision. The Bible teaches otherwise:

"Now that you have purified yourselves by obeying the truth so that you have sincere love for your brothers, *love one another deeply, from the heart*" (1 Peter 1:22).

"Above all, *love each other deeply*, because love covers over a multitude of sins" (1 Peter 4:8).

What do you think Peter has in mind—love as a decision? love as resolve? love as commitment? These things are important, but we have emphasized "love is something you do" so much that we have forgotten some key biblical teachings about love:

- Love feels. It is a matter of the heart.
- Love wants to draw near, to get close.

Love is the real me connecting with the real you. No masks. No hiding. No pretending. Christian love is the real me connecting with the real you as we represent God to each other. We normally think of ourselves as ambassadors of Christ representing God to a world that does not know him (2 Corinthians 5:20). But it is also true that we are Christ's ambassadors to one another. We represent God to each other.

Christianity is all about drawing close. It is about a God who, in his triune state, models closeness. It is about a God who created people to bear the image of this closeness. It is about a God who drew close by walking with the first man and woman in the Garden of Eden. It is about a God who drew close by actually becoming one of us. Hebrews 4:15 states, "For we do not have a high priest who is unable to sympathize with our weaknesses, but we have one who has been tempted in every way, just as we are—yet was without sin."

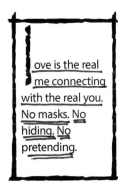

ove is the real me connecting with the real you. No masks. No hiding. No pretending.

Christianity is about people drawing close to each other in love. Yet many churches are characterized more by polite distance than by the connection of hearts and souls in love. Disciple-making teachers recognize the need to create environments where deep friendships, friendships like the ones my friends and I experienced in college, can develop. Disciple-making teachers understand that friendships such as these won't develop on their own. Disciple-making teachers know that they will need to be very intentional in helping to develop close friendships.

So how do we help people develop these kinds of friendships? We *teach* and *model* the characteristics of true love, of true friendship. We help them discover and understand that a friend is…

* **F** un to be with,
  R eal (not superficial),
  I nterested and interesting,
  E ncouraging,
  N ice and (when needed) not nice, and
  D ependable.

Dependable friends are hard to find, but dependable friendships can be developed over time. As people draw closer to one another in heartfelt love, as they share the fun of each other's company, as they become real with their successes and struggles, as they grow interested in each other's lives and interesting to each other, as they encourage and cheer on one another to their full potential, as they demonstrate Christian love by being nice most of the time but not nice when they must—they will form intimate and dependable relationships that can stand the tests and the trials of time.

Do you have any relationships like that? More important, is your group made up of friends like that? Teachers don't create disciples on their own. Disciples are made within the context of a body. They are made within the context of relationships that can happen in small groups. This is why the first I of the DISCIPLES acrostic is so key. It is the job of the disciple-making teacher to see that it happens.

Self-Esteem

✳ Self-image is much like a thermostat that controls a person's behavior. External forces may attempt to push behavior in one direction or another, but self-image ultimately decides what a person does. Consequently, people rarely live above the level of their self-esteem. They tend to live consistently with their perception of who they are. People who see themselves as sinners tend to behave as sinners. People who see themselves as saints tend to behave as saints. People who see themselves as world-changers tend to turn the world upside down.

Knowing this, disciple-making teachers work from the inside out. They encourage people to change the way they act by changing the way they see themselves. Disciple-making teachers challenge people to abandon inaccurate views of themselves and to embrace God's view of them. They encourage people to see themselves as God sees them.

If we are disciples of Jesus, we will believe that we are God's beloved (1 Thessalonians 1:4), saints (Ephesians 1:1), children of God (Ephesians 1:5), aliens and strangers (1 Peter 2:11), servants of God (1 Peter 2:16), heirs (Titus 3:7), salt and light (Matthew 5:13-16), and the righteousness of God (2 Corinthians 5:21). We will also live in a way that reflects our true identity as disciples.

In this discussion, we will explore three of these biblical identity statements. This isn't the entire picture, to be sure, but it should be enough for us to understand what a difference a biblical self-image can make in our lives. By examining what the Bible says about who we are, we will become better able to develop the self-image of a disciple of Jesus Christ.

The Beloved

Two times during the ministry of Jesus, the windows of heaven opened up and the Father spoke audibly to Jesus and everyone around him, saying, "This is my Son, whom I love" (Matthew 3:17; 17:5). Apparently God, in his infinite wisdom, knew that from time to time Jesus needed to be reassured and reminded of his Father's love. Every now and then, Jesus needed to hear his Father say, "You are my beloved Son" (Mark 1:11b, TLB). I suspect the people you teach need to be reminded as well.

Interestingly enough, Paul uses the same Greek root to describe God's attitude toward us. In 1 Thessalonians 1:4, Paul states that all Christians are "loved by God." We are, quite simply, God's beloved. God's love for us is one of the basic truths of the gospel. It is one of the first things we teach our children in Sunday school. Children who don't know very much about God still sing, "Jesus loves me, this I know, for the Bible tells me so." God's love for us offers a common theme in our songs and in our sermons.

Unfortunately, many Christians don't *feel* all that loved by God. They don't see themselves as God's beloved. They feel as though God is either disappointed in them or has forgotten about them altogether. They may believe on some detached, intellectual level that God loves them, but they don't feel it in their hearts. If we want to create disciples, we will constantly remind people that they are the beloved of God.

We are often awed by impressive people, but we generally love only those people whom we feel love us. I might be impressed by movie stars, athletes, or business people, but I usu-ally don't come to love those people unless I have personal contact with them and sense that they care for me. In the same way, we can be impressed with God whether or not we feel that he loves us. But we will only love God to the degree that we are convinced that he loves us. We will only live as God's beloved to the degree that we feel loved by God.

Our hymn books often contain various love songs to God, but God also has love songs written to us. Zephaniah 3:17 states: "The Lord your God is with you, he is mighty to save. He will take great delight in you, he will quiet you with his love, he will rejoice over you with singing." Imagine! The God of the entire universe who created the stars with the command of his resonant voice rejoices over you with singing! The God of the entire universe loves you and takes delight in you. If that doesn't cause you to smile, you may want to check your pulse.

> **We will only love God to the degree that we are convinced that he loves us.**

Do you see yourself as someone who is beloved by God? Better yet, do you *feel* that you are the apple of your Father's eye? Do the people you teach feel that they are God's beloved? If not, I invite you to pray right now and tell God you want to exchange whatever belief you have about yourself for the truth that you are the beloved of God. Then I would encourage you to lead your class to do the same. Until their self-image is one of being loved by God, they will never behave as children of God.

Saints

In addition to describing us as God's beloved, the Bible routinely refers to us as saints. In fact, "saints" is one of the most frequent titles applied to Christians. Here are just a few examples:

> "Paul and Timothy, servants of Christ Jesus, to all the *saints* in Christ Jesus at Philippi, together with the overseers and deacons" (Philippians 1:1).

> "I pray that you, being rooted and established in love, may have power, together with all the *saints*, to grasp how wide and long and high and deep is the love of Christ" (Ephesians 3:17b-18).

> "Paul, a servant of Christ Jesus...to all in Rome who are loved by God and called to be *saints*" (Romans 1:1a, 7a).

Unfortunately, most of us feel more than a little uncomfortable with the word. To discover what I mean, ask your class members to introduce themselves to the group by saying, "Hi, I am Saint Josh" or "My name is Saint Susan." Then ask them how it felt. I'll bet it made them feel uncomfortable. People today are simply not used to being referred to as saints. They don't think of themselves as saints.

Saints are not people so pious and good that their feet don't touch the ground when they walk. The biblical word for "saint" refers to something or someone who is separate or different. Imagine a basket of apples. If you pulled out several apples, they would be separate from the rest. In a very real sense, they would be "saint" apples. This is the core meaning behind the biblical word "saint."

As saints, we have been separated from the world in general into a distinct group called the Church. Consequently, we are to live separately from sin and separately from the ways and thinking of the world. Have you seen those pictures where everything in the picture is black-and-white except for one small detail? To draw the viewer's attention to a rose, a car, or a small child, the creator of the picture colors that one detail and leaves the rest of the picture black-and-white. This is what it means to live separately, to live as saints. Our lives should stand out within our gray world just as the color image stands out against the black-and-white background in the picture.

If we find that believers are not living separately, that they are following the ways of the world rather than the ways of Jesus, we might need to check their self-image. People's outer lives tend to reflect their self-image, and they generally live as saints only to the degree that they see themselves as saints. Disciple-making teachers help their students become comfortable with the concept that they are saints. They teach and model what it means to be "in the world but not of the world" (see John 17:15-19). They encourage the people in their groups to live lives that stand in distinct contrast with the ways of the world, to live lives of grace, kindness, love, and righteousness.

The Righteousness of God

If you are in a room where you can do so, say this out loud: "I am the righteousness of God." How does it sound? Does it make you feel uncomfortable? Does it seem a little hard to believe? If so, you might consider memorizing this verse, "God made him who had no sin to be sin for us, so that in him we might become the righteousness of God" (2 Corinthians 5:21).

Christ died on the cross to take on the penalty for our sin and thus to make us the righteousness of God. This is what happens in salvation. It is also what is supposed to happen in our daily lives. Unfortunately, all too often it doesn't.

Instead of asking for too much, we settle for too little. We ask people to live pretty good lives and to be reasonably responsible citizens. But this isn't God's standard. God commands us: "Be perfect, therefore, as your heavenly Father is perfect" (Matthew 5:48).

In *The Pursuit of Holiness,* Jerry Bridges quotes 1 John 2:1a: "My dear children, I write this to you so that you will not sin." Bridges rightly points out that John does not say, "I write this so that you will not sin very much" or "so that you will cut down on sinning." Rather, John states that he wrote what he did so that we do not sin at all. That is God's standard: that we not sin at all.[4]

A while back, a friend and I were discussing why so many single, dating Christians don't remain sexually pure. During the course of our conversation, my friend mentioned a mutual acquaintance: Joe, a single Campus Crusade for Christ minister. "Only people like Joe can seem to remain sexually pure," my friend noted. "Do you know why Joe is sexually pure, while others are not?" I asked. "Because Joe sees himself as the righteousness of God. That is his identity, who he is. To live impurely would be incongruent with how Joe sees himself."

Living as God's righteousness—which we will never do perfectly—starts from the inside. We must see ourselves as the righteousness of God so we can live as the righteousness of God. As long as we see ourselves as sinners trying to behave like righteous people, we will probably not make much progress. But if we view ourselves as God views us, as the righteousness of God, we will begin to live in a manner consistent with our identity.

Disciple-making teachers encourage people to see themselves as God sees them and then help people to live out their identities every day of their lives. The three identity statements in this discussion—the beloved, saints, and the righteousness of God—are merely a few examples of how God's Word describes who we are. Disciple-making teachers will commit themselves to introducing the people in their classes to other biblical identity statements on a regular basis. One statement you might consider is found in Acts 16:14: "One of those listening was a woman named Lydia, a dealer in purple cloth from the city of Thyatira, who was a *worshiper* of God. The Lord opened her heart to respond to Paul's message." Jesus' disciples are worshipers of God, which is the subject of the next discussion.

Corporate Worship

Much of what it means to be a church happens in small groups and the relationships formed in those small groups. Worship is an exception. The larger the group, the better the worship. The worship that takes place when the entire body gets together and really celebrates God is seldom duplicated in a small group. Worship is one aspect of church life that generally gets better and better as the group gets larger and larger.

Of course, meaningful worship simply doesn't happen on its own. So disciple-making teachers help their class members form true and informed appreciation of worship. They explain that God is the audience of our worship, that we are not the audience of an onstage performance. They encourage the group to be more concerned with pleasing God in worship than with how well they are pleased with the music or the sermon.

In a sense, worship should be among the least self-serving things we do. Worship is, by definition, for God and not for us. Ironically, however, we often talk about whether or not *we* got something out of worship. That is beside the point. The whole point is worshiping God, not coming to a show where we can be entertained. Instead of asking ourselves, "Were we entertained?" we should ask, "Did God feel worshiped?"

Doing so would probably go a long way toward settling the debate about styles of worship. Churches today offer a number of worship styles: traditional, contemporary, gospel, blended, and so on. But this shouldn't give us the idea that we are doing this to cater to our own preferences and tastes. Worship is not about what we like; it is about what God likes, and he is more concerned with the state of our hearts than he is with the style of our worship. I believe that God loves variety enough that he is pleased when people worship him with Bach as well as with rock. However, we must never forget that variety in worship is not to cater to our tastes. It is to effectively bring people with various tastes together to worship God.

So how should we worship God? When the Samaritan woman asked Jesus this question, he replied, "God is spirit, and his worshipers must worship in spirit and in truth" (John 4:24). Because we are to worship God in spirit *and* in truth, teaching and worship should go hand in hand. Teaching provides the content behind worship, while worship gives expression to what has been learned. Worship at its best gets very specific. It

> Worship is, by definition, for God and not for us. Ironically, however, we often talk about whether or not *we* got something out of worship.

tells God specifically what we like about him. Not content to mindlessly repeat, "I love you. I love you. I love you," true worshipers go on to explain why they love God.

True worshipers know and understand the attributes of God. They rehearse them often in private worship, which provides a foundation to their public worship. Even when their mouths are merely saying, "I exalt you. I exalt you. I exalt you," their minds are filling in the blanks. In their hearts they are saying: "I exalt you because you are all-powerful, because you came near in the person of Jesus, because you know the answers to every dilemma, because you sovereignly watch over the entire world, because you can make all things work together for good."

Although I am a big believer in contemporary worship services, I do see a problem with some contemporary worship at this point. Many contemporary songs simply do not have the same depth of meaning and content as many of the two-hundred-year-old songs in our hymn books. I grow a little weary of songs that say nothing more than, "I will praise you. I will praise you. I will praise you." My heart thirsts to worship God in spirit *and* in truth, to sing songs with content, to sing songs such as this one. Read these verses slowly. If you know the tune, pause to sing it quietly:

> O sacred head, now wounded, with grief and shame weighed down,
> Now scornfully surrounded with thorns, thine only crown;
> How art Thou pale with anguish, with sore abuse and scorn!
> How does that visage languish which once was bright as morn.
>
> What thou, my Lord, hast suffered was all for sinners' gain.
> Mine, mine was the transgression, but thine the deadly pain;
> Lo, here I fall, my Savior! 'Tis I deserve thy place;
> Look on me with thy favor, vouch-safe to me thy grace.
>
> What language shall I borrow to thank thee, dearest Friend,
> For this thy dying sorrow, thy pity without end?
> O make me thine forever! And should I fainting be,
> Lord, let me never, never outlive my love to thee.[5]

Singing a song such as this does something for me that "Praise you, praise you, praise you" doesn't. Singing a song such as this helps me worship God in truth. It challenges me to love God with my mind.

The same principle holds true between lovers. They don't merely say, "I love you." They tell each other why they love each other, specifically what they appreciate about each other. He talks about her eyes, her intelligence, and her spiritual strength. She talks about his hair, his character, and his heart for God. Praise at its best is in the details. In the same way, our worship of God should be full of spirit and truth.

Disciples cannot be created in the classroom alone. There is something about coming into God's presence in corporate worship that does what no classroom experience can do. Disciple-making teachers encourage their class members to seek God in corporate worship, in honest worship full of spirit and truth.

Intimate Family Life

Many books on discipleship pretend that we don't have families. They talk about Scripture memory, spending time alone with God, sharing one's faith, and other important issues, but for some reason they have little to say about family life.

Lance Witt and I fell into this trap when we originally worked out the DISCIPLES acrostic. Family life was not included. When I first mentioned this to Lance, I suggested that we lump family life under "Intimate Friendships." "Families are friends," I explained. Lance wisely argued for a different approach: "Yes, but family life is too important. It must be given the priority in the acrostic that it has in real life." I think he is right.

Everyone gives lip service to the importance of family: "God first, family second, and everything else after that." But we say it too quickly. I'm not sure we are really convinced that our second most important responsibility in all the world is to cultivate an intimate relationship with our families. The evidence would indicate otherwise.

IS THAT THE TRUTH IN MY FAMILY ?

Too many men merely aspire to be reasonably good, respon-sible Christian husbands who pay the bills, stay out of other women's beds, and never even mention divorce. They reason that if they don't bring the subject up, they can be sure that it won't happen to them. This makes as much sense as thinking that if you never say the word "cancer," you will not ever get it. The recovery literature has a word for that: denial. This approach will never do.

* The Christian commitment to marriage involves much more than merely resolving not to get divorced. It requires us to make having an incredible marriage one of the greatest passions of our lives. The discipleship books need to tell us this. Where is all that Bible study and prayer supposed to lead, if not to help us become better people—better husbands, wives, parents, and children? That should be a top priority.

VERY TRUE !

I don't need to spend a lot to time convincing you that families are in trouble, do I? You know the statistics. Recently the statistics were vividly brought home to me as my wife was looking through

> **The Christian commitment to marriage involves much more than merely resolving not to get divorced.**

an old picture album. Three out of the four couples in one picture are now divorced.

To make matters worse, many (if not most) of the marriages that don't end in divorce aren't all that happy. All too often couples stay together because he can't afford to move out, because she is afraid, because he doesn't want to be away from the kids, or for any one of a hundred reasons. None of these reasons has anything to do with the fact that they want to spend their evenings together. Still, they stay together—miserable. No one is in any deeper pain than the person whose family life is failing.

John 17 records Jesus' prayer for himself, for his disciples, and for us. Three times in this prayer, Jesus prays for his followers to be unified. I have italicized these requests so you can spot them easily from the lips of Jesus:

> I will remain in the world no longer, but they are still in the world, and I am coming to you. Holy Father, protect them by the power of your name—the name you gave me—*so that they may be one as we are one.*
> —John 17:11

> I have given them the glory that you gave me, *that they may be one as we are one:* I in them and you in me. *May they be brought to complete unity to let the world know that you sent me* and have loved them even as you have loved me.
> —John 17:22-23

✷ Oneness is important to Jesus; unity matters to God. Where do we imagine this oneness will be displayed if not in Christian homes? Someone once said the best testimony to the existence of God is a halfway decent Christian marriage. But how much better testimony a great marriage would be. I believe that we should seek to develop incredible marriages. We were created in the image of a triune God who enjoys a perfect relationship. We were created to follow God's relationships in our marriages.

Back in the Garden of Eden, God looked at a perfect man in a perfect environment with a perfect relationship with him and said, "It is not good for the man to be alone. I will make a helper suitable for him" (Genesis 2:18). Life in a perfect environment was not good, when it was a life alone. Humans were created for community. This community is displayed first and foremost in Christian marriage.

Look again at John 17:22-23, this time observing the underlined portion. Do you understand the significance of Jesus' words? It is almost as though Jesus is turning to the world and saying, "If my people don't love each other, you have my permission to believe that I didn't come." Jesus made a similar statement a little earlier: "By this all men will know that you are my disciples, if you love one another" (John 13:35). So I ask again, if this love is not evident in the homes of the people we are teaching, where then do we look for it?

＊ If we can produce disciples who have great families, we will have a great testimony with non-Christians. If we don't, it's unlikely that they will ever hear us. Jesus admitted as much. In fact, our most effective strategy for growing churches may be to produce husbands and wives who love each other passionately.

The opposite is also true: Nothing damages the reputation of the church more than marriages that are failing one way or another. Non-Christians seem to understand intuitively that if Christianity really is true and it truly makes a difference, then that difference would be seen first and foremost in a Christian home. Most non-Christians recognize the incongruity of a bad Christian marriage.

This is not a book about family life, and space does not permit me to explain in detail what it takes to create a solid marriage and a great family life. I do want to spend some time, however, on the teacher's role in creating great families.

Teaching people how to create healthy families is not something teachers should do once in a while. Rather, they should include it in nearly every lesson. The home is the first arena in which truth is to be applied, so teachers should point out how a biblical text applies to life in the home just about every week. Whether the group is studying Isaiah 55, the Sermon on the Mount, or Ephesians 6, there should be some application to family life. In addition, teachers ought to regularly dedicate specific lessons or class times to family and marriage concerns. Most pastors present series on these types of issues every year or two. Disciple-making teachers should do the same.

> If we can produce disciples who have great families, we will have a great testimony with non-Christians. If we don't, it's unlikely that they will ever hear us.

Disciple-making teachers don't pretend to have all the answers on marriage and family issues. Rather, they encourage group members to seek the advice and assistance of those with the experience and expertise necessary to deal with complex relational issues. At times this means recommending books or articles that address someone's specific needs. Disciple-making teachers also encourage people to attend conferences and retreats that focus on family and marriage issues. They demonstrate the value of such experiences by attending themselves from time to time. Finally, disciple-making teachers are aware of and can recommend counselors when someone in the class requires individualized help.

Disciple-making teachers challenge group members to hold each other accountable with regard to their families. They encourage people to get together weekly and ask each other the hard questions about their marriages and their families. As iron sharpens iron, class members sharpen each other. This may be the most important contribution that small groups make to families.

Disciple-making teachers also do what they can to hold group members accountable. They know that, like many forms of cancer, family problems are curable if caught early, so they don't just deal with family issues when a crisis occurs. They regularly engage in preventative work. They don't just operate an ambulance service at the bottom of the cliff; they build fences at the top. They are not nosy, but they are concerned and discerning. They watch for little signals that tell how a couple is doing. They notice body language and the little comments that a couple makes, whether to each other or about each other. Sometimes they ask the couple directly how their marriage is doing. They notice the relationship that parents have with their children.

Most important, disciple-making teachers give priority to their own families. They teach by word and by example. They practice good family disciplines such as a weekly date night, one-on-one times with their kids, and an occasional overnight trip away from the kids. They read about family issues themselves and are constantly evaluating and improving their family lives.

This is not some Stoic discipline for them. It is life. There is nothing they would rather do than sit for hours on the couch and talk with their husband or wife—unless it is to play ball or go on a hike with their kids. They not only love their families, they *like* them.

Disciple-making teachers work to develop good family lives for themselves and for the people in their classes. But they do not condemn those who do not have good family lives. Unfortunately, not every disciple has a strong marriage or family. Some disciples do all they can, but for some reason they cannot achieve the goal of a great family. They want to. They try to. But perhaps because their spouses don't want to, or because they were scarred by dysfunctional families in the past, or because they are suffering for mistakes they made in the past, or because one of their children is rebelling, or for some other reason, their home is not a happy place. We can't always control that. We only control what we do. Disciple-making teachers recognize that and encourage the people in their class to develop as healthy a family life as they possibly can.

Building strong, intimate family relationships is one of the primary tasks of disciple-making teachers. Do you remember the other things we are trying to build into our students?

D _____

I _____

S _____

C ORPORATE WORSHIP
I NTIMATE FAMILY LIFE
P assion for God
L ay ministry
E vangelistic interest
S acrificial giving

Passion for God

The human soul craves adrenaline—something to get excited about, something to get on our feet about, something that will cause us to wake up, something that will get us going, something that will get us out of the easy chair and into the game of life, something worth living for.

Sports exist to satisfy this need for adrenaline. We love the thrill of victory and the agony of defeat because even in defeat we can savor the sweet taste of adrenaline. The entertainment industry also exists to satisfy the human thirst for adrenaline. Romances, action movies, suspense dramas, science fiction pictures—all are created to pump adrenaline in one form or another into our systems.

To be honest, much of the thrill of sin has to do with adrenaline. "Stolen water is sweet; food eaten in secret is delicious!" states Proverbs 9:17. And it isn't just watermelons that taste sweeter when you eat them secretly behind the barn. Kisses seem sweeter, too. Talk to someone who has fallen into an extramarital affair. That person will probably tell you that the risk of getting caught made the sexual pleasure all that more exciting. Our souls crave that adrenaline.

I remember when I was a kid, I stole a pack of BB's from a Gibson's department store. It wasn't that I wanted to save the fifty-nine cents. It had nothing to do with money. It was about adrenaline. It was about the sweetness of stolen watermelons or, in my case, stolen BB's. It was about the thrill of seeing what I could get away with, pushing the edge, taking chances. It was about drinking deeply from the fountain of adrenaline. Our souls crave it.

the human soul craves adrenaline.

Normally, we try to combat this craving with one word: Don't. Don't do this; don't do that. This approach seems logical, but it is as unbiblical as it is ineffective. The Bible teaches that "Don't" tends to increase our desire to do whatever it is we're not supposed to do. Paul explains, "But sin, seizing the opportunity afforded by the commandment, produced in me every kind of covetous desire. For apart from law, sin is dead" (Romans 7:8). In other words, "You just gotta check the wet paint for yourself." When someone tells me not to touch the paint, something within me yells, "Touch it!" When you tell me "No!" everything within me screams "Yes!"

This is why the Bible offers a different solution. Paul tells us, "Do not be overcome by evil, but overcome evil with good" (Romans 12:21). In the context in which we are speaking, we could say, "Overcome bad passion with good passion." Don't merely say "no" to your evil impulses. Say "yes" to something bigger, more exciting, more exhilarating. Say "yes" to a passionate relationship with God because knowing God is more adrenaline-producing than anything else on earth—even stolen watermelons.

Instead of telling people, "No! No! No!" we should ask them, "What do you really want?" Christian teaching and worship should help people get in touch with their deepest spiritual desires and then call them to pursue those desires.

For example, ask a Christian man involved in an affair what his soul most deeply craves. He will probably tell you that he desperately wants to relate deeply with someone, to be loved and accepted, to be connected emotionally with another person. In all likelihood, he will also admit that he would prefer to do that in committed marital relationship and that not being able to realize that desire is his greatest regret in life.

So how do you help someone caught in this trap? Some Christians would confront this person and say, "Don't. You shouldn't, so just stop." Christianity at its best would come alongside this person, get him in touch with his God-given *spiritual* desires, and then challenge him to settle for nothing less.

There is a certain legitimate self-interest in Christianity at its best. One reason we want to follow Christ is because it is the only way we can satisfy our souls' deepest desires. The deepest desire of the human soul is to touch the face of God. Stolen kisses simply cannot compare. Moreover, only the thrill of connecting with the Almighty will be sufficient motivation in the long haul to keep us from sin. Only deeper passions can overcome lesser passions, so we must overcome our evil desires by cultivating even stronger good desires.

One of the most controversial articles in the history of Leadership Journal was an anonymous article written by a pastor who fought against an addiction to all kinds of pornography. Talk about passion! The article contained so much steamy passion that some readers protested that this wasn't healthy reading for Christian leaders. The writer tried everything to control this passion gone awry. He wanted desperately to tame the wild horses within him. He was miserable, but he simply could not overcome his passion by looking at sin and saying "no." "Just say no" just didn't work for him. It was not until he turned around and realized what he was missing that he was able to escape his sin. One day, he wrote, he realized that the coolness of the ocean spray on his face didn't touch him anymore. His soul was dying. You wouldn't think that missing a little ocean mist would keep a sex addict straight, but it wasn't about ocean mist. It was about the hunger to experience God and life in all its fullness. When this pastor got in touch with this inner craving, he was able for the first time to walk away from his addiction. In other words, the best way to overcome bad passion is with good passion.

Consider the alternative: creating dull people. Too many churches are content to create dull people these days, but God doesn't want people to be dull. God wants us to be passionate—people who drink regularly and deeply from the adrenaline that knowing God, and only knowing God, can produce.

We will never reach the world with dull, bored people. Only people with adrenaline can get the job done. Consequently, we need to fill people's souls with adrenaline every time we gather together. I am not talking about personality. I have learned from incredibly sedate teachers whose hearts throbbed with adrenaline. And after listening to them, mine did as well. I have also known teachers who yelled and screamed but failed to move me. Passion springs from the deepest part of our souls. How it expresses itself will vary from disciple to disciple.

Similarly, worship with no adrenaline is a disgrace to God. God doesn't want people who are bored with him. Again, I am not talking about a particular worship style or any other external factor. I am talking about the heart. We can feel just as much adrenaline when we sing a staid old hymn as when we sing a peppy chorus. The key is to sing both with a heart full of passion for God.

So how can we develop passion for God, the kind of passion that will enable us to overcome the evil passions that tempt us? Read the words of this "old hymn" for the answer:

> Turn your eyes upon Jesus,
> Look full in his wonderful face,
> And the things of earth will grow strangely dim
> In the light of his glory and grace.[6]

> **The best way to overcome bad passion is with good passion.**

Here is the answer: Only looking in the face of Jesus will cause the things of this earth to grow strangely dim. "Don't" and "should" and "ought" never will. Both in our teaching and in our worship, we need to lead people to tap into their souls' deepest desires. There is within each of us a great water source that can burst forth like an artesian well and spread life into every corner of our lives. We simply need to tap into that source. We spend too much time at the hand pump. We need to tap into the reservoir.

> **W**orship with no adrenaline is a disgrace to God.

Disciple-making teachers get people in touch with their deepest passion—their passion for God—by constantly turning their eyes upon Jesus and the life that springs from him. Unfortunately, all too often we content ourselves with creating dispassionate, bored Christians. Of this, John Piper writes,

> The irony of our human condition is that God has put us within sight of the Himalayas of his glory in Jesus Christ, but we have chosen to pull down the shades of our chalet and show slides of Buck Hill—even in church. We are content to go on making mud pies in the slums because we cannot imagine what is meant by the offer of a holiday at sea.[7]

What kind of people are you producing?
Tin soldiers?
Good folks?
Nice people?
Hard workers?
Good church members?
People of passion?

Never forget the P in the DISCIPLES acrostic. Without it you only have puppets and pharisees. We are about creating people of heart, people of adrenaline, people of passion.

Lay Ministry

In my opinion, we talk about spiritual gifts too much these days. Granted, the gifts are important; they are taught in the Bible, and we should teach about the gifts along with everything else. But gifts are not above all other issues. They are certainly no more important than cultivating a heart of love and a willingness to serve regardless of one's giftedness.

Understanding gifts is, in the long run, a means to an end. The goal of teaching about gifts is to get people involved in ministry in the area of their giftedness. The goal of teaching about gifts is to get people involved in ministry in the area of their giftedness. I said that twice because it is important.

Which would you rather have: someone who knows what his or her spiritual gift is, who can explain, analyze, and distinguish that gift from every other gift, but who is not involved in ministry; or someone who says, "I dunno what my gift is—I just love people," and who is waist-deep in ministry?

Of course, we shouldn't have to make that choice. I would prefer to work with people who can say without hesitation or pride, "My gift is..." *and* who are actively ministering in the areas of their giftedness. That is the best. But if I have to choose between someone who understands the doctrine of gifts and someone who is involved in helping people live better lives, I will choose the latter every time. The teacher in me would like to see the former as well, but the Great Commission depends on the latter.

The process of getting people involved in lay ministry always starts with a relationship with God. People must follow God before they are ready to minister to others. Consequently, disciple-making teachers constantly "push" people toward God and allow him to "push" them into ministry. This is, after all, a biblical model. Isaiah, for example, encountered God and then said, "Here am I. Send me!" (Isaiah 6:8b). In the same way, Jesus first called the disciples to follow *him* and then promised to make them fish for people (Matthew 4:19). All too often, however, we reverse the process by trying to put people to work before they truly encounter God.

That is why our appeals to ministry should start with the person, not with the organizational chart. Instead of starting with the chart and trying to fill all its slots, we should start with the people, push them toward God, and see how many ministry slots God pushes them into. If every teacher and small-group leader would do that, I doubt that we would have many slots to fill.

The simplest way to nudge people into ministry is to challenge them to use their gifts to grow the group. Most gifts operate within the context of relationships that form in small groups. Consider the following list of spiritual gifts from Romans 12:7-8. Check the ones that apply to small groups.

- Serving
- Teaching
- Encouraging
- Contributing
- Leadership
- Showing mercy

Obviously, all these gifts can be exercised in contexts other than a small group, but every one of them can and should be used regularly in our small groups.

For example, one woman in one of our small groups calls every member every week to ask what she can pray about. That is ministry. That is what being the Body of Christ is all about. One member of that class told me that she really wanted to change to a class at a different time but she just could not bring herself to do it; she felt cared for by this lady. It matters not that we don't have a label for her gift. All that matters is that she is ministering. We should make heroes out of such people. They deserve recognition (1 Corinthians 16:18b).

Because most lay ministers are recruited personally, disciple-making teachers need to sit down one-on-one with each person in the group and challenge him or her to consider a specific ministry. Don't push the issue if it is not the right ministry or the right time, but challenge group members individually on a regular basis.

For example, you might sit down with a couple or an individual and say…

> Could you help me by serving as our group's outreach leader? We need someone to keep up with potential members and invite them to class. You would need to invite them to every social and special event we have; just keep inviting them until they tell you to stop. You know, most people who are opposed to the gospel are not opposed to ice cream.

or…

> We need a fellowship leader, and you are the most fun-loving couple I know. Would you be interested in helping us plan something fun to do together about once a month? It's a key part of building the kind of community we want to create.

or…

> I've noticed that you guys seem to like having people in your home. I don't know if you ever thought about this as a ministry or not, but it really can be. What would you think of opening your home several Friday nights a month to two or three couples from class and a new couple or two? I'll work with you the first time or two, and we can just try it out for a while. I have a feeling we will see some good results and have fun in the process. Does that sound like something you would be interested in doing?

For too long we have told people, "Love God and go find something to do." My experience indicates that most people need more direction than this. They need to be personally challenged to ministry. They need someone to sit down beside them and say, "I believe in you. I think you can do it. I want to ask you to try."

Most of us don't go to restaurants and simply tell the waiter what we want to eat. We choose from a menu, even when we know the kind of food the restaurant serves. The menu helps us decide what to eat. Wouldn't it be a bit frustrating to go to a restaurant and have the waiter say, "Just tell me what you want. Our cook can fix anything"? In the same way, disciple-making teachers serve people well by saying, "Here are six areas of ministry. Do any of these fit your area of giftedness?" This is much better than suggesting that they go find *something* to do.

But we shouldn't limit our vision merely to our classes or small groups. In most churches, the ministry with the greatest need is working with kids. Knowing this, disciple-making teachers should challenge people to consider working with preschoolers, children, or youth. People should have to make a conscious decision *not* to work with kids. Because the need is so great and so continual, it should always be our first concern. Disciple-making teachers also make sure that class members serving in children's ministry are always invited and included in fellowships. We should go the extra mile to ensure that everyone remains a vital part of the group.

because most lay ministers are recruited personally, disciple-making teachers need to sit down one-on-one with each person in the group and challenge him or her to consider a specific ministry.

Disciple-making teachers also encourage class members to look beyond the four walls of the church. They challenge people to start creative new ministries that meet the needs of neglected people. They try to tap into the creative and entrepreneurial spirit that God has put into the hearts of his people. They cheer people toward their visions, no matter how outrageous those dreams might seem. They remind people that Promise Keepers, a nationwide ministry for men, was started by a lay minister, a football coach.

Disciple-making teachers believe God can do great things through ordinary people, so they constantly give ownership of the ministry away. They recognize that ownership is the key to motivation. People don't wash rental cars. So when class members take responsibility for class outreach and fellowship, disciple-making teachers don't micromanage those lay ministers' efforts. They may hold their hands at first, if people want and need it, but eventually they release people to own their own ministries.

In the same way, when class members see the need for a new ministry, disciple-making teachers don't assume the responsibility to make it happen. Rather, they firmly and honestly tell people, "You got an idea? You got a job." They don't allow for "upward-leaping monkeys." Rather, they keep the monkey squarely on the back of the people responsible for the ministry. If someone drops the ball, they watch it bounce. They treat adults as adults.

Ultimately, we want to create "world Christians," people with a heart for the world. Disciple-making teachers love to see group members involved in short-term mission projects. They secretly hope that God will someday call a full-time missionary from the group. Consequently, disciple-making teachers take seriously the command to pray that God will send laborers into the harvest (Luke 10:2). They know they cannot recruit people to ministry or motivate them to stay with it unless God is working in their lives, so they ask the Holy Spirit to call people to ministry.

As devoted as they are to encouraging people into ministry, however, disciple-making teachers recognize that not everyone is ready for ministry at all times. They let people rest. They accept people who are broken. They let people get well. They ask people to serve, but they make it easy to say "no." They feel a sense of urgency about getting people into ministry, but they are not compulsive about it.

We will never win the world through professional ministers. We must give the ministry to lay ministers. The best way to do this is for those already in ministry to recruit others to the ministry. We must continually pray to the Lord of the harvest to send workers. We must release ownership of ministry to those who will step up to the plate and take their turn at bat. We must cheer on the entrepreneurial spirit of those who would start new ministries. We must give people specific ministry options from which to choose. We must encourage and support those who are ministering. We must remember the ministries for our children.

Making disciples involves far more than just making good people. When we encounter God, we meet a God who is up to something. God has an agenda, and everyone who meets him gets to join in his work. That is why lay ministry is a part of the DISCIPLES description of discipleship. Do you remember the rest?

D _____
I _____
S _____
C _____
I _____
P _____
L _____
E vangelistic interest
S acrificial giving

Evangelistic Interest

Our outreach strategy needs to take seriously the notion that some Christians have a gift for evangelism while others do not. Paul writes, "It was he [Christ] who gave some...to be evangelists" (Ephesians 4:11). Every Christian has a place in the disciple-making process, but not everyone needs to be on the front line.

Suppose we were a specialty hospital whose sole business was helping mothers give birth. Even if this were the single focus of the hospital, not everyone would actually deliver the babies. In addition to doctors and nurses, hospitals need accountants, janitors, laundry personnel, security people, kitchen workers, and on and on. Though the purpose of the institution would be to provide childbirth services, only a small percentage of the workers would actually deliver babies.

This analogy applies to the church with one important exception: The purpose of the church is not to have spiritual babies. Our purpose is to make disciples. We seek to create mature, growing Christians who love God with all their hearts, souls, minds, and strength. In fact, to clarify this analogy, we might say that, since our purpose is to produce mature adults, providing "childbirth" services is only a first (albeit necessary) step in the process.

Unfortunately, too many churches view themselves as specialty hospitals whose only purpose is to bring spiritual babies into the world. But Juan Carlos Ortiz rightly rejects this view and challenges us to stop promoting the eternal childhood of the believer.[8] We are neither simply a childbirth center nor an emergency clinic. Rather, the church is a full-service health care center that provides traditional hospital care for those who need it *and* exercise and diet programs for the well. Our purpose is not just to have babies or to help the sick. We should also help the healthy get healthier.

Therefore, although we need everyone involved in the evangelistic process, we don't need everyone in the spiritual delivery room. Peter Wagner points out that if the average church had only 10 percent of its members each seeing one or two people come to faith every year, that church could barely keep up with the task of making disciples out of these new Christians.[9] Statistically, he is right. A church of two hundred members would have twenty evangelists. If each one of these led one to two people to Christ each year, this church would add thirty new people every year. Most churches with two hundred members would have a hard time assimilating and discipling thirty new Christians every year. That church couldn't afford to have 90 percent of its people involved in evangelism. They would be needed in the discipling part of the process. We need the 90 percent to teach, love, encourage, lead, care for, and disciple these new Christians. In short, the need of the hour is to get everyone involved in the disciple-making process in the area of his or her giftedness.

We need people devoted to the ministry of evangelism, people who want to be on the front line seeing non-Christians bow their heads and hearts before God, people who constantly remind the church of its evangelistic calling, people who train and release those with the gift of evangelism. We don't need everyone to be an evangelist, but we do need some to use their God-given gifts in this ministry.

On the other hand, people with the gift of evangelism also need to recognize that not everyone is gifted as they are. They need to relax and let others minister in other ways. The realization that they are among the few gifted to do evangelism should fuel their zeal to do the work rather than fuel their agitation with those who don't have the zeal. In sum, people with the gift of evangelism should spend more time trying to reach non-Christians and less time haranguing Christians who have neither the gift nor the calling of evangelism. If they did, both groups would be happier and more productive.

Knowing all this, disciple-making teachers are consciously aware of the need to draw out the evangelists in their group. They ask the Lord of the harvest to send workers from their group into the fields that are ready to be harvested (Matthew 9:38; John 4:35). They come alongside individuals who appear to have the gift of evangelism and challenge them to consider this strategic ministry. Disciple-making teachers allow gifted individuals to experiment and to grow, perhaps by giving them the responsibility of being the group outreach leader. They also encourage these lay evangelists to look beyond the group to the opportunities that the larger body provides. Finally, disciple-making teachers cheer the efforts of the evangelists and challenge them to develop their skills for maximum effectiveness.

Still, no one is allowed to be blasé about evangelism. If some in the group regard evangelism with apathy or boredom, the disciple-making teacher regards that as a serious problem of the heart. Not everyone needs to be on the front line, but everyone should have a heart for the front line. God rejoices in the presence of the angels whenever one sinner repents (Luke 15:10); how much more should God's people rejoice to see non-Christians come to faith in Christ?

Not only should we all be interested in evangelism, we should all be prepared to participate in it. Peter commands us, "Always be prepared to give an answer to everyone who asks you to give the reason for the hope that you have. But do this with gentleness and respect" (1 Peter 3:15b). To help people be prepared to share their faith, you might want to conduct evangelism training during your class or small-group meeting. This will help encourage everyone in the group to be interested in, prepared for, praying about, and looking for opportunities to share their faith.

Finally, a biblically based evangelistic interest extends beyond one's local area. Christians are to be kingdom-focused. Therefore, disciple-making teachers seek to create people with the world on their hearts—people who give to, pray for, and are deeply interested in missions; people who love to hear what God is doing around the world; people who recognize that the Great Commission extends far beyond their own personal Jerusalem. If you aspire to be a disciple-making teacher, you need to have a clear picture of your ultimate goal *and* a clear understanding of what you need to do to reach it. The DISCIPLES acrostic describes what we are trying to create: disciples of Jesus Christ. To reach that goal, we will have to cultivate an evangelistic interest within each and every member of the group.

Sacrificial Giving

Which do you think comes first: loving God or giving to God's work? I used to think that loving God comes first, that when people fall in love with God, they naturally give out of the overflow of their lives. I used to think that…until I read Matthew 6:20-21 a little more closely.

Jesus said that our hearts will be where our treasure already is (Matthew 6:21). Of course, the heavenly treasures Jesus speaks of in verse 20 are not limited to money, but Jesus' words do relate to our finances. In other words, Jesus taught that our hearts follow our checkbooks, that our affections will go where our money goes. Knowing this, disciple-making teachers encourage people to love God more deeply by challenging them to give more sacrificially.

There's a second reason that teaching people to give is crucial. It really *does* matter in the real world of ministry. There is a direct correlation between the amount of money people give and the amount of ministry the church is able to do. The more money a church has to work with, the more it is able to do in terms of reaching people and making disciples out of them.

Why do you suppose that every church doesn't have an aggressive ministry to singles, senior adults, and a dozen other groups? Money. Most churches don't have any philosophical or theological objections to calling a singles minister, but many churches do have a problem providing him or her with an ample ministry budget. The same holds true for a dozen other ministries in churches like yours and mine. The more we give, the more ministry we are able to do.

In Ephesians 4:28, Paul commands thieves to stop stealing and to do something useful with their hands instead. Few churches hesitate to teach that. Paul goes on, however, to explain why former thieves (and presumably all Christians) should work: so that they may share with those in need. In other words, one reason we work is to enable us to give our earnings to meet the needs of others. Giving not only deepens our love for God and enables us to minister to others, it also invests our day-to-day work with purpose.

Disciples of Jesus also open their wallets to a variety of causes because giving is not a one-shot deal for them. They give generously, sacrificially, and proportionately month after month, year after year. They welcome the chance to kick in a little extra when a kid wants to go to camp or when a special offering is taken for a music group that comes to town. Disciples don't really keep score on such things. They are just happy to do their part.

Of course, when people cannot give at all, God doesn't want them to feel guilty about it. Attitude is as important as action. Disciples with a giving attitude will often wish they could do more, but they recognize and are at peace with what they can and cannot do. They don't feel guilty about what they cannot give; they are just happy to give what they can, when they can. In fact, they regularly deny appeals for gifts because all they can do is all they can do.

> Jesus taught that our hearts follow our checkbooks, that our affections will go where our money goes.

On the other hand, disciples of Jesus try to live in such a way that they are able to give on a regular basis. They try to control their lifestyle so that they have money to share with the needy. They keep debt to a minimum. They guard their hearts against becoming overly enamored with the trinkets of this world. As a rule, they don't drive the latest cars or live in the biggest houses.

Recognizing that disciples of Jesus should be characterized by sacrificial giving, disciple-making teachers encourage their people to give in various ways. Most important, disciple-making teachers present a positive example of cheerful giving. They personally know the satisfaction of giving, and they share with the group how giving has deepened their love for God.

Disciple-making teachers are not shy about talking directly about giving, either. They expose the group to biblical passages on giving just as they are and allow people to feel the full weight of those texts. They challenge people to apply what is taught in specific, tangible ways. Principles of giving are some of the simplest biblical truths to apply, so disciple-making teachers challenge group members to give as they can and should. They do not seek to protect the wallets of the people in their groups.

Some non-Christians are turned off by churches that talk a great deal about giving. They perceive these churches as being primarily interested in money. Because of this, sometimes we neglect to teach what we should. Money is not our only concern, but it is part of the disciple-making process. Paul put it into context for us when he said, "But just as you excel in everything—in faith, in speech, in knowledge, in complete earnestness and in your love for us—see that you also excel in this grace of giving" (2 Corin-hians 8:7). This is what disciple-making teachers try to do: to encourage people to excel in all things, including giving.

Teachers hold a significant advantage over pastors in teaching about giving. First, teachers have no self-interest in asking people to give because none of the money comes their way. Ministers don't have that luxury. In addition, teachers can ask the group how they feel about their giving. They may not want to ask class members to share personal details in class, but they can ask questions such as…

d isciples with a giving attitude will often wish they could do more, but they recognize and are at peace with what they can and cannot do.

- "Do you think you are close to where you ought to be as far as giving is concerned?"
- "How do you determine how much to give and how often to give to God's work?"
- "If we collected a special offering, how would you decide how much to give, if anything?"
- "What are your life's goals and dreams with regard to giving?"

In time, you will probably learn to know some in the group well enough that you can actually ask about their giving practices and tell them about yours. Friends talk about such things. Friends spur each other on in the disciple-making process.

Giving involves far more than mere money, however. Giving is an attitude, a way of life. Disciples also give of their time, their attention, and their affections. They give of themselves. They do not seek to grab all they can out of life. Rather, they contribute to making this a better world.

Sacrificial giving is not peripheral to living the disciple's life. It is central to the lifestyle that the Holy Spirit is trying to produce in every Christian. It is one of the key traits that should characterize disciples of Jesus. Do you remember the eight other characteristics? By now, we should know them all.

D
I
S
C
I
P
L
E

S

Now that we have a clear picture of what we are trying to create through our teaching, we are ready to discuss what needs to happen in class within the learner in order for the disciple-making process to be successful.

Notes

[1] *The Spirit-filled Christian* (Colorado Springs, CO: NavPress, 1977), 47.

[2] Lynne and Bill Hybels, *Rediscovering Church* (Grand Rapids, MI: Zondervan, 1995), 199–200.

[3] Francis Schaeffer, *No Little People* (Downers Grove, IL: InterVarsity, 1974).

[4] Jerry Bridges, *The Pursuit of Holiness* (Colorado Springs, CO: NavPress, 1978), 190.

[5] "O Sacred Head, Now Wounded," words attributed to Bernard of Clairvaux.

[6] "Turn Your Eyes Upon Jesus," by Helen H. Lemmel.

[7] John Piper, *Desiring God* (Portland, OR: Multnomah Press, 1986), 83–84.

[8] Juan Carlos Ortiz, *Disciple* (Carol Stream, IL: Creation House, 1975), 85.

[9] C. Peter Wagner, *Your Spiritual Gifts Can Help Your Church Grow* (Ventura, CA: Regal Books, 1979), 177.

Section Two:
The Learner in Class

	Outside of Class	In Class
Teacher	Preparation	Presentation
Learner	Lifestyles	Learning

Barriers to Learning

> U nless the room temperature is above sixty-five degrees, it is unlikely that learning will take place.

Unless the room temperature is above sixty-five degrees, it is unlikely that learning will take place. If, however, the temperature rises above eighty degrees, learning probably won't take place either. God has made us "amphibious" beings, with one foot in the spiritual world and one foot in the physical world. We are not merely spirits who happen to inhabit bodies, nor are we bodies with spirits attached. We are spirit-bodies, amphibious beings not totally complete without both elements (2 Corinthians 5:1-4). The spirit aspect influences and affects our bodies. Likewise, our bodies affect various spiritual processes, including learning. That's why we generally do not learn unless the room temperature is roughly between sixty-five and eighty degrees.

The Physical Environment

This is not only true of the temperature. A number of things in the physical environment can impede or even kill learning. Maybe adults should be mature enough to rise above these, but most of us are not. Unless the physical environment is right, the right things usually do not happen in class for the disciple-making process to progress.

Temperature is among the most important of the physical factors in the classroom. Another is the quietness of the room. It is difficult for learning to take place when there is a screaming baby next door, a loud video across the hall, or yelling teenagers in the hallway. People ought to be able to filter these distractions out, but loud, distracting noise usually aborts the learning process. No matter how fervently you pray or how well you prepare your lesson, it is unlikely that learning will take place if there is a wailing baby in the room next door. On the other hand, if your group is watching a video, it must be loud enough for everyone to comfortably hear.

Everything in the physical environment either contributes to or distracts from the learning process. Hard chairs tend to distract from the learning process. Little piles of junk—last quarter's Sunday school books mixed with a few maps and some discarded Bibles—tend to distract from learning. On the other hand, an attractive, quiet, well-decorated room with comfortable chairs tends to increase the chances that the right things will happen with the learners in class. Attractive art and tasteful wallpaper tend to help people relax so they can concentrate on the business of learning. If people's bodies are relaxed, their spirits—their minds and hearts—can learn.

Likewise, arranging chairs in a circle encourages people to talk to each other, whereas placing them in straight rows tends to limit discussion. People are simply not comfortable talking to those whom they cannot look at face-to-face. When the chairs are set in straight rows, the best we can expect is for conversation to take place between the class members and the teacher. If we want people to talk to each other, we need to arrange their chairs in a circle.

Physical factors—the arrangement of the chairs, the temperature of the room, the presence or absence of various distractions—all of these affect learning.

Teacher-Learner Relations

A comfortable physical environment is not the only prerequisite to learning. Emotional and social issues are equally important. For example, people don't learn well from people they do not like. They will tend to notice the teacher's mistakes and be uninspired by his or her brilliance. On the other hand, people will generally lap up every word spoken by a teacher they adore. We learn best from the teachers we like most.

Likewise, it is difficult to learn from someone we are angry with. I have listened to brilliant lessons led by people who had irritated me, and I remained unmoved. This is why Jesus placed such emphasis on relationships. Jesus taught that if you are driving to church and remember you promised to return your neighbor's lawn mower, the same lawn mower that is still sitting in your garage, you should turn around and take care of it (see Matthew 5:23-24). In short, relationships matter to God.

Because of this, teachers should seek to be well-liked, not for their own sake, not because they like to feel popular, but because people learn best from the people they like best. This principle, of course, could be taken too far. There is such a thing as loving human praise more than the praise of God. That is not what I am advocating. Rather, I am talking about serving God by obeying the command to "live at peace with everyone" (Romans 12:18). Jesus and Paul enjoyed enormous popularity, but both had their enemies.

So how do you live in such a way that people like you and are therefore willing to learn from you? First and most important, you must genuinely love and be interested in the people in your class. We tend to like people who seem to like us and take an interest in our lives. According to 1 Peter 4:8, "Love covers over a multitude of sins." If we truly care about people, they will know it, and they will tend to forgive us our mistakes. On the other hand, no matter how personally charismatic a teacher might be, we will not be drawn to someone who seems uninterested in or cold toward us.

Likewise, we tend to be drawn to people who obey the command to "be kind and compassionate to one another" (Ephesians 4:32). This includes being courteous and polite. If you want people to come to your class or small group, be nice to them. Sometimes we forget this. We teach our children to memorize this verse and then flagrantly violate it as adults.

Finally, teachers should seek to establish rapport with learners. Rapport is the feeling of having something in common with someone. When we learn that someone grew up in the same small town that we did, we have immediate rapport. Ultimately, our rapport is based on the fact that we have a common faith, but skilled teachers look for things that accentuate their rapport with learners. They try to find things they have in common. Paul said he had become all things to all people so that by all possible means he might be able to save some (1 Corinthians 9:22). Skilled teachers try to do the same. They try to find and develop as much common ground with their class members as they can.

> If you want people to come to your class or small group, be nice to them.

With some people, we will struggle to find anything that we have in common. This is one reason we need to reproduce new groups: so we can offer to people a number of small-group opportunities in which they can find rapport. If you, as a farmer, disciple an engineer and then start and turn over a new group to that engineer, you have done more than create a new group. You have created a new opportunity for other engineers to find rapport. That teacher and that group will be more likely to reach other engineers than you ever would. The more groups we have, the better positioned we are to reach more people and more kinds of people.

The future of the church depends on creating a variety of groups because we simply cannot become everything to everyone. Computer people like to become disciples under the teaching of other computer people. Outdoor types like to learn from people who have backpacks in their garages. Construction workers prefer to be discipled by someone who knows the difference between a doorjamb and a doorknob.

If we want to maximize our impact on learners, we must seek to live at peace with all of them. We must love, be polite to, and find rapport with them. If learners are not at peace with the teacher, it is unlikely that the right things will happen in class for them to become disciples of Jesus out of class.

Learner-Learner Relationships

Learners need to be at peace with the teacher, but that is not all. They also need to be at peace with each other. Relational rifts are educational killers, and learning generally does not take place in an environment where the members of the group are angry with one another.

Of all the people who currently do not attend church, 85 percent did attend church for a prolonged period of time.[1] In short, most of the "unchurched" used to attend church. Of those who did, most probably left because of a relational issue. They became angry with someone and left. People generally do not leave churches over critical theological issues. Rather, they generally leave because of relational problems that are not handled with effective people skills.

Nearly every church with which I consult needs help teaching members how to get along with each other. Churches everywhere are filled with people who disagree with each other and do not know how to effectively and lovingly communicate those disagreements. Every pastor should preach at least one series of sermons a year to help people learn to get along. Every Sunday school teacher or small-group leader should give major attention to helping people to get along. Too many churches claim to be hothouses of love, when, in fact, they are cesspools of gossip, anger, pettiness, and the like.

No matter how well the teacher prepares or presents the lesson, people rarely learn in an environment of conflict. Relational rifts within the class kill the disciple-making process. Effective teachers recognize this and thus help learners to get along with one another. Paul, for example, asked a leader in the Philippian church to help two members who were struggling to get along: "I plead with Euodia and I plead with Syntyche to agree with each other in the Lord. Yes, and I ask you, loyal yokefellow, help these women who have contended at my side in the cause of the gospel" (Philippians 4:2-3). Paul asks this unnamed "yokefellow" to help these women get along. I believe God would ask every Sunday school teacher and small-group leader to do the same. Jesus stated, "Blessed are the peacemakers" (Matthew 5:9). He recognized that peace simply doesn't happen on its own, that we need to promote it in whatever way we can.

For learning to take place, we must create a positive learning environment. Uncomfortable or distracting physical settings, cold or unloving teacher-learner relations, and squabbles between class members will all kill the learning process. Yet there is one more obstacle we must overcome to create a disciple-making learning environment.

Teaching in a Storm

It is difficult for people to learn when the storms of life rumble in and crush their lives into piles of rubble. There is little a teacher can do about this. As much as we want something to happen in class in the lives of learners, they will not be impressed by our lesson on the Second Coming if they are preoccupied with the possibility of a job loss or a divorce.

Recently a public school teacher told me the sad story of one of his students who had been killed in an automobile accident. He reported that he was almost completely unable to teach for the next several days because the class was preoccupied with their recent loss. External situations and struggles affect people's moods. Troubled learners may not be able to concentrate on the subject at hand. We cannot control that, but we can be aware of it.

On the other hand, sometimes people experiencing trouble are unusually teachable. Often those rare teachable moments come in the middle of a storm. In some ways, we may have a better opportunity to alter the trajectory of a would-be disciple's life during a dark time than during any other time. Our teaching, however, must be personalized to the individual. People will not listen to a *generic* lesson in the middle of a storm, but they will be extra receptive to a message personalized to their needs.

Disciple-making teachers know their class members well enough to recognize when they are hurting. They care enough to listen and, when appropriate, present what the Bible has to say to the broken and wounded at their point of need. Disciple-making teachers make the most of these teachable moments, but they also know that not every moment is for teaching. There is a time to teach and a time to be silent. There is a time to give a warm hug and a time to bring a warm casserole. People need good teaching, but they need good friends as well. They need someone to listen to them, someone to meet their physical needs, someone to love them. They need someone to come alongside and ride through the storms of life with them.

In order for the right things to happen with the learner in class, the teacher must provide a physical environment that is conducive to learning, develop positive relationships with the people in class, and promote healthy relationships between class members. In addition, the teacher needs to know what is going on in the life of each learner and, when possible, to present a personalized lesson tailored to the situation of someone going through one of life's storms.

It takes more than a good environment and good relationships for disciple-making to take place. Still, these preliminary issues must be addressed. If we do not get them right, we may not have the opportunity to lead people to become disciples. Assuming that we do have these things right, the next discussion will show us exactly what must happen in class with learners in order for us to make disciples.

The Learning Process

Teachers can use a variety of techniques. They can ask questions, present lectures, facilitate creative learning experiences, or use a number of other teaching methods. The point, however, is not what the teacher does. It is what happens inside the learner as a result of what the teacher does. Regardless of one's teaching technique, these seven things must take place for disciple-making learning to happen:

1. The learner must become interested in the lesson.
2. Truth must become truth that matters to the learner.
3. The learner must discover how this truth relates to Monday morning.
4. The learner must recognize the gap between his or her life and the life God calls us to live.
5. The learner must see the benefits of obedience and the drawbacks of disobedience.
6. The learner must commit to exchange one belief, value, attitude, or behavior for another.
7. The learner must be held accountable for his or her decisions and commitments.

Let's look at each of these in greater detail.

> The point is not what the teacher does. It is what happens inside the learner as a result of what the teacher does.

1. Getting Their Attention

Why do people come to class? Because they are thirsting for God "in a dry and weary land where there is no water" (Psalm 63:1)? I don't think so. In fact, if they are coming for that reason, it's likely that they are already living the disciple's life and actually need to be released to ministry. You don't need to worry too much about the people who come thirsty to know God. They are already well on their way to becoming disciples. But what about the rest of the people who are in class: Why are they there?

- Some people come because their spouses make them.
- Some singles come to meet potential dates.
- Some come to talk with their friends.
- Some are curious and want to learn more.
- Most probably come out of sheer habit.

For whatever reason they come, most people have something on their minds when they arrive. We are not writing to blank screens. We are trying to transform already occupied minds. The first thing we must do, then, is to break people's preoccupations. Put simply, we must get their attention.

Getting people's attention, however, is anything but simple. Many of the would-be disciples in our group are as preoccupied as the stereotypical husband with his nose in the sports page. In fact, you might try visualizing your group sitting down for class, each with a newspaper in front of him or her. Simply remember that the main difference between that image and reality is the newspaper, not the level of preoccupation. Some are preoccupied with the fight they had on the way to church or with how they will pay their bills. Perhaps someone is trying to figure out how to sit by the girl he's flirting with, while she is trying to stay as far away as possible. Someone else, tired of goo-gooing with her two-year-old all week, may be looking forward to some adult conversation. Still someone else is undoubtedly bored with the thought of another lesson. Whatever the cause of people's preoccupations, your task remains the same: Get their attention.

The classic example of a communication medium that fails to do this is the airlines' message about what to do if the plane starts to crash. One would think, on the surface, that people might be fairly interested in this…but they're not. They pay little attention to this message. If the airlines really wanted to get people's attention, they would actually let those oxygen masks drop down now and then. They might even let the air out of the cabin as the masks drop. This would break the preoccupation barrier. As it is, everyone is totally preoccupied with other things. No one listens; no one learns.

So how can we break the preoccupation of people whose minds are a million miles away? One approach is to have people answer a question as they introduce themselves. I always ask group members to state their names unless I know that every single person there knows everyone else. If you are doing well at outreach, you will regularly have new people who do not know everyone else. It is a real courtesy to them to have group members introduce themselves every week. This is also an excellent time to get people interested in the lesson. For example, you might ask people to introduce themselves and to answer a question such as these:

- "When was a time that you were really frightened?" (This works well if the lesson deals with fear.)
- "On a scale of one to ten, how would you rate your relationship with your parents?" (This question strikes a balance between being personal enough to be interesting without being so personal that it makes people feel uncomfortable.)
- "Let's imagine that, like a cat, you had nine lives: What is one totally outrageous thing you would do with one of those lives? Maybe jump out of an airplane? explore the jungles of South America? be a professional athlete? What would you do if you had three extra lives with which to do something outrageous?" (People really enjoy answering this question!)

Asking people to answer a thought-provoking or off-the-wall type of question is one way to break their preoccupations, but it is not the only way, and it is not guaranteed to work. You might also begin by telling a captivating story, reading an interesting quote (and asking people to respond to it), or recounting an amusing incident. One of the worst ways to begin is to ask everyone to open to a biblical text and to read from it. Larry Mays often writes a snappy lesson title on the board. For example, in a recent lesson on Job, he wrote, "When life tumbles in, what then?" A title such as this captures people's attention because it applies to their Monday mornings. A title such as "Job's troubles" would not break people's preoccupations.

Another teacher, Darla Hapgood, used another creative method to introduce the middle section of Job. (It is not the most fascinating or easily applicable material.) She assigned one speech to several of the people in her class, who were then responsible to explain what was in that speech. Talk about getting their attention! Darla turned one of the least interesting sections of the Bible into one of the most interesting lessons all year. That is what getting people's attention is all about.

Yet another teacher I know often plays a video—even an excerpt from a recent movie—to introduce the lesson topic. I have seen other teachers use object lessons to create interest or actually get the group physically involved. In short, there are a multitude of ways to get people's attention. Your job is to be as creative as you can to get the attention of the class right from the beginning.

One approach that can be used in conjunction with those mentioned thus far is the "promise." The promise is also a reliable way to communicate the central idea of the lesson and keep the lesson on target.[2] I encourage you to read the following paragraphs carefully. If you use the promise in your teaching, you will have greater focus and impact than ever before.

Sometimes people learn too little because we try to teach too much. The promise helps us avoid that by focusing people's attention on the central idea of the lesson. What I am suggesting is that early in the lesson, you take the central idea you want to teach and offer it to the class in the form of a promise. For example, you might start class with promises such as these:

• "Today we will explore the biblical admonition not to worry. If any of you would like to worry less than you do, stay with me and I will show you how to cut your worrying in half, maybe more."

• "Getting along with others is one of the most important skills that anyone can possess. So today we are going to learn some key biblical principles that, if applied, can help you get along with just about anyone."

• "For years I struggled with really internalizing the concept of God's unconditional love for me. Doubts about God's love plagued me for a long time, but eventually I came to a sense of peace about it. Today I want to share with you how you can experience that same peace and assurance of God's love."

The promise seeks to answer a single question for the listener, "Why should I listen?" It is an effective way to capture people's attention and to focus their minds on the lesson topic. Use it often.

2. The Truth Will Set You Free

Once we have people's attention, we must confront them with the truth. Truth that is eternal and transcendent must become truth that matters. Lots of things are true, but most of them don't matter all that much. For example, it doesn't matter to me that water boils at 212 degrees at sea level or that the area of a circle is equal to πr^2. Both of these facts are true, but they really don't matter to me. In the same way, it may not matter to your class that...

• Isaiah was an eighth century prophet of Israel.
• The New Testament was written in Koine Greek.
• The preeminent mark of a disciple is love.
• Love means being patient with and kind to others.

All these statements are true, but until people realize how these truths matter to their real lives, they will not be changed toward becoming DISCIPLES on Monday morning.

Specifically, learners need to see three things: the Bible, their own lives, and the connection between the Bible and their lives. All too often, we study the Bible in order to derive truths or ideas from it, then teach those ideas. But I believe that people need to connect with the Bible itself. Learners needs to actually see or even read out loud a portion of a biblical text that relates to their lives on Monday morning. How helpful it is for someone to read, "love is patient; love is kind" (1 Corinthians 13:4a) and then ponder, "Am I patient and kind with my kids?" In most cases, the truth that matters most to people is the truth that they discover for themselves. (Actually, God reveals it.) The truth that matters most is the truth that comes in "aha" experiences when they see how the Bible connects with their real lives.

This is part of the miracle of teaching would-be disciples. People without God's Spirit are spiritually blind and thus cannot see how the truth of God's Word relates to their lives (1 Corin-thians 2:14; 2 Corinthians 4:4). But the Holy Spirit enables Christians to really see the truth so that it becomes truth that matters. This is why Paul said, "I pray also that the eyes of your heart may be enlightened in order that you may know the hope to which he has called you, the riches of his glorious inheritance in the saints" (Ephesians 1:18). Just as Paul prayed for God's Spirit to open the eyes of the Ephesian Christians, disciple-making teachers should ask God to open the eyes of the people in their class.

The teacher is completely dependent on the Holy Spirit to do what the teacher can never do. Only the Holy Spirit can illuminate God's Word so that transcendent truth becomes truth that matters. But the Holy Spirit often uses people with the gift of teaching to lead people into God's Word, to confront them with eternal truth. The Holy Spirit will do his part, but the teacher must do his or her part as well.

Disciple-making teachers learn how to sense when the Spirit is moving within the group. They "listen for the Wind" that tells them the Holy Spirit is working. They pray, study, and plan to create that moment. They pause as the Holy Spirit touches people's hearts and minds. The moment passes, but they can see the effect in changed lives. Teaching is about creating moments in which the Holy Spirit illuminates the Word of God through the guidance of a Spirit-led teacher. Wise teachers sense, savor, and use these moments to the glory of God.

3. Learning Involves Application

The moment of illumination, however, is not enough. In addition to recognizing transcendent truth as truth that matters, the learner must discover how that truth applies to his or her Monday morning. This can take one of several forms. Sometimes people will discover that the Bible (not just the teacher or a principle) is calling them to live a certain way. Or they may realize that God wants them to hold certain beliefs or to have certain attitudes. Application is not limited to behavior. Sometimes it involves our emotions, our attitudes, or our beliefs. If someone walks into class feeling unloved by God and walks out feeling loved by God, learning has taken place. Learning involves application.

The Bible must connect to people's lives, their Monday mornings. It must connect to what they do every day of the week. Even if they don't understand all of the whys and wherefores, they should understand what they are to do, what they are to believe, or what they are to feel. They need to understand what the eternal truths of the Bible look like in real life.

They need to be like the man who came home from church one day and, when he was asked by his wife what the sermon was about, replied, "I don't know that I can say." "Well, what Scripture text was it based on?" "I dunno." "Can you remember the main idea?" "Nope." "Well, how about the stories or illustrations?" "Can't say that I recall…But you know that scale we have out back, the one that doesn't weigh things correctly? We need to get it fixed." We might wish that this man had remembered more, but at least he understood what he was to do. In fact, if I had to choose between people remembering a lesson and understanding what they should do, I would choose the latter every time. Learning is about application.

4. Recognizing the Gap

Once people understand how God's Word applies to their everyday lives, they are ready to confront the gap between where they are and where they should be. For authentic learning to take place, people must clearly see the gap between the behaviors, attitudes, beliefs, and emotions that they have and those that God calls them to have. Before people can change, they must recognize not only where they should be but also where they actually are. They must see that there is a difference between the two.

The two most common biblical words for sin are archery terms. They describe an arrow "falling short of its target." There is a gap between the center of the target and where the arrow landed. In the same way, there is a spiritual gap (sin) between where we should be and where we actually are. Recognizing this gap leads us to repent. Admitting this gap causes us to change.

How different this is from what I have seen happening in small groups and Sunday school classes over the years. In my opinion, we could summarize too many discussions in two words: "Yup, yup."

"Yup, yup, the world sure is awful."

"Yup, yup, we sure have it together."

"Yup, yup, too bad others aren't like us."

"Yup, yup, we are doing just fine."

This kind of discussion does not change lives. It does not create disciples. This kind of discussion defends, rather than challenges, the Christian status quo. In order to apply God's Word to their lives, people must recognize that they are not where they should be.

One reason we try to avoid seeing the gap is because we associate it with condemnation. We reason that if, in fact, there is a gap—if we have sinned—then condemnation must follow. But condemnation was taken care of at the cross. There is no condemnation for those who believe in Christ Jesus (Romans 5:1). Consequently, we are free to explore the gap in an atmosphere of grace.

Unless people experience the gap in an atmosphere of grace, they will probably not accept it. Two thousand years of Old Testament history demonstrate that the method of law and condemnation does not work. We are more likely to live as saints when we are accepted as sinners.

Unfortunately, sometimes when we *talk* about grace, people still *hear* the message of condemnation. Subtleties of our body language, our intonation, and our facial expressions betray our real feelings. To avoid this, disciple-making teachers meditate on grace often and are careful to expose people to the gap only within an atmosphere of grace.

Still, disciple-making teachers believe in the gap. They teach for the gap in every lesson. Every question, every explanation, every comment points to the gap. They guide the discussion in light of today's gap. The set the gap before the group in large fluorescent letters. They make sure that no one misses the gap. They realize that making disciples requires them to point out the gap between where people are and where they ought to be.

We will never arrive at perfection, but we must always strive for perfection (Matthew 5:48). There is always a gap between where we are and where we should be. In fact, sometimes it will seem as though we are shooting at a moving target. As soon as we arrive at one level of discipleship, we will discover a higher level for us to seek. Unfortunately, many churches are content simply to produce reasonably good Christians they can leave alone. People arrive at a moderate level of biblical knowledge, commitment, and service—then stay there for the rest of their lives. Sad to say, many churchgoers have neither seen nor felt a gap in years.

Let me ask you: Is there a gap between how you teach and how you should teach? Are you a disciple-making teacher who helps people recognize the gaps in their lives every week?

5. Obedience Pays...In the Long Run

Simply put, people are motivated by self-interest. Every human on planet Earth constantly asks, "What's in it for me?" (This is often referred to as the WIIFM factor.) Moreover, people generally look at self-interest in two ways: What are the benefits of obedience? and what are the drawbacks of disobedience? Pleasure and pain are the two classic human motivators. So like it or not, disciple-making teachers must use the carrot and the stick to nudge people along.

The Bible has a great deal to say about carrots and sticks, about the benefits of obedience and the drawbacks of disobedience. For example, the Bible teaches that God "rewards those who earnestly seek him" (Hebrews 11:6). Other verses also speak to the issue of rewards:

• "You, O Lord, are loving. Surely you will reward each person according to what he has done" (Psalm 62:12).

• "Misfortune pursues the sinner, but prosperity is the reward of the righteous" (Proverbs 13:21).

• "He who is kind to the poor lends to the Lord, and he will reward him for what he has done" (Proverbs 19:17).

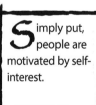
Simply put, people are motivated by self-interest.

• "When you give to the needy, do not let your left hand know what your right hand is doing, so that your giving may be in secret. Then your Father, who sees what is done in secret, will reward you" (Matthew 6:3-4).

• "For the Son of Man is going to come in his Father's glory with his angels, and then he will reward each person according to what he has done" (Matthew 16:27).

Observe that rewards are based on works, on obedience. Salvation is based on grace. Discipleship is based on grace. Rewards, however, are not given on the basis of grace. They are earned on the basis of works.

In many ways, obedience is its own reward. Jesus taught that he came to bring us abundant life (John 10:10a). We live an abundant life as we live obediently to God. Abundant living is the reward for obedience. Conversely, Jesus also taught us that the evil one came to "steal and kill and destroy" (John 10:10b). The evil one seeks to punish us and ruin our lives. Consequently, submitting to God is in our best self-interest. Obeying God brings the good life. Disobedience results in the evil one killing, stealing, and destroying the good life.

Ultimately, reward and punishment are based on two different fates: heaven or hell. Obeying the command to repent and trust in God's forgiveness leads to eternal life in heaven. Refusing to accept the gift of God's acceptance results in everlasting punishment. The contrast couldn't be more stark. All in all, disciple-making teachers have a great deal to work with in terms of presenting the rewards of obedience and the drawbacks of disobedience.

Some would argue that speaking of punishment and reward misses the point of the gospel altogether. Some believe that appealing to rewards and punishments is appealing to the very self-interest that Christianity would wish to destroy. Some would say that our goal is to produce people who have no self-interest and are thus unmoved by the appeal of rewards, people who neither think of themselves nor want for themselves. This is a misguided approach.

As I noted earlier, the Bible says a great deal about rewards and punishments. We would not be true to the Bible if we failed to teach this. The Bible does not tell us to be good whether or not it is good *for* us. Being good is always, in the long run, good for us. There is no conflict of interest between what is good for me and what God wants for my life.

The deceiver would confuse us at this very point. Many people see the dichotomy as follows: the good life on one side and the "should life" on the other. On one side is all the fun stuff that I would like to do and that would make my life pleasurable. On the other is the stuff that I ought to do, none of which is all that much fun.

To be honest, this is often true…in the short run. Sin has its pleasures, but only for a season. It is more pleasurable in the short run to operate a car without paying attention to certain maintenance issues. It's a bit messy to check the oil and to make sure that the water level in the radiator is as it should be. To "sin" by neglecting to do these things may make today more pleasant, but it can make tomorrow miserable. It's the same in the spiritual realm.

Knowing this, disciple-making teachers recognize the pleasure of sin but accentuate its consequences. They emphasize the rewards of obedience, which are many. The evil one seeks to do the opposite, to accentuate sin's pleasures while placing the benefits of obedience in the distance.

Self-interest is a powerful motive, so disciple-making teachers do not try to work against it. Rather, they harness self-interest and point it in the right direction, which is to please God. Disciple-making teachers work hard to convince people that the obedient life is the best life they can possibly experience. The "good life" is not the world's to offer. Only God can promise *and* provide the good life, the abundant life—life to the full.

God would give us pleasures that this world can never match. God would cause us to rejoice in him, to find pleasure in him that would cause this world's fare to pale by comparison. God would give us a magnificent feast at his banquet table, whereas this world can only offer crumbs. God would fill our hearts with unending joy, if only we would not be so quickly satisfied with the glitter and chrome that quickly fades. Disciple-making teachers motivate their students to live the good and obedient life by painting in bold colors the benefits of obedience and the drawbacks of disobedience.

6. Committing to Change

Recognizing the need to change and how it relates to life is not enough. Seeing the benefits of obedience is not enough. People must also make the decision and the commitment to change. The biblical word for this is repentance, which means to change one's mind.

For a long time, repentance carried emotional overtones for me that were all wrong. I felt that repentance meant, "You are bad, so you need to say you are sorry." A call to repentance sounded like a message of condemnation. I'm glad to report that I have repented of that belief. I now see repentance as a change of belief, behavior, or attitude. Repentance is not about condemnation. Condemnation has no place in Christian living. As Paul wrote, "Therefore, there is now no condemnation for those who are in Christ Jesus" (Romans 8:1). Repentance is not about condemnation; it is about change. Repentance is the heart and soul of what it means to become a disciple.

Teachers should regularly encourage people to repent. Because we are simply calling on people to change, we can do this in a rather matter-of-fact way. Whenever we encounter a belief or an attitude that is contrary to God's truth, we should encourage people to repent of that belief or attitude. We should not be afraid to smile at someone and say, "I call on you to repent of your doubts about God's love." Of course, we should also talk freely about the beliefs, attitudes, and behaviors that *we* have repented of. Admitting that we sometimes need to repent of wrong beliefs and actions will make it easier for others to do so when they are called on to change.

Repentance is not merely saying you are sorry. Being sorry is not enough. Repentance is a U-turn. If you were trying to drive north and mistakenly got on the freeway going south, being sorry about making the wrong turn would not be enough. Repentance is making the U-turn so that you're headed the right way.

In a thousand little turnings, we change from a sinner to a saint, from a rebel to a lover. Repentance *should* be a regular event in the life of every Christian. It *must* be a regular event for those who seek to become disciples of Jesus. Repentance is something that should happen in class because teaching is all about change. If we are not calling people to repent, we are not making disciples; at best, we are merely filling people's heads.

7. Accountability

Most of us need to be reminded of our commitments. This is why we wear wedding rings and celebrate our anniversaries. It is why the bank sends us a coupon book that lists our scheduled car or house payments. Good intentions, however well meaning, do not usually produce the desired results unless they are accompanied by some sort of accountability. Consequently, disciple-making teachers will devise a way to hold everyone in the group (including the teacher) accountable to do what he or she has committed to do.

Since I have already discussed accountability in some depth (see pages 19-20), I will limit my discussion here to several key points. First, there is a limit to how much we can hold people accountable in an "open" Sunday school class. A group seeking to maximize its evangelistic efforts must limit its in-class accountability. If it doesn't, newcomers might feel out of place. Closed accountability groups often take people deeper in discipleship but provide limited usefulness in outreach. Both types of groups serve the kingdom of God.

Second, there should be some sort of accountability in all kinds of groups, even open or evangelistic ones. One way to promote accountability is to encourage the formation of out-of-class accountability groups. That way group members will hold each other mutually accountable to do what they've committed to do.

Another approach is to ask people to share their successes from the previous week. For example, a teacher might ask...

• How did last week's lesson affect the way you lived this past week?

> Teachers should regularly encourage people to repent.

• How did you apply our last lesson on the need to be honest in all our dealings?

• Did anyone have a meaningful time alone with God that you can tell us about?

This last question is especially useful. Because anyone can get on board within a week, it is fairly nonthreatening to newcomers. At the same time, it holds the entire group accountable for one of the most important traits of a disciple: disciplined in daily life. We need to model both in our lives and our lessons the idea that it is normal for all Christians to spend time each day in prayer and Bible reading.

In order for disciple-making teachers to be effective, seven things need to take place:

1. The learner must become interested in the lesson.

2. Truth must become truth that matters to the learner.

3. The learner must discover how this truth relates to Monday morning.

4. The learner must recognize the gap between his or her life and the life God calls us to live.

5. The learner must see the benefits of obedience and the drawbacks of disobedience.

6. The learner must commit to exchange one belief, value, attitude, or behavior for another.

7. The learner must be held accountable for his or her decisions and commitments.

Most books on teaching concentrate on what the teacher must do, and we will turn to that next. But please note that this section, not the next, is the real point. What the teacher does matters far less than what the learners do as a result of what the teacher does.

At the same time (and this is fairly obvious), the teacher cannot do just anything to achieve the desired results with the learner in class. He or she must plan strategically and execute reasonably well to accomplish the seven steps of the learning process. Ultimately, teachers only control what they do, but they should always seek to do what they can to produce the desired results in the minds, hearts, and lives of their learners.

Notes

[1] George Barna, *Evangelism That Works* (Ventura, CA: Regal, 1995), 50.

[2] Calvin Miller, *The Empowered Communicator* (Nashville: Broadman & Holman, 1994), 75.

Section Three:

The Teacher in Class

	Outside of Class	In Class
Teacher	Preparation	Presentation
Learner	Lifestyles	Learning

Asking Good Questions

In order for the right things to happen with learners in class, the teacher needs to do the right things in class. Asking good questions is one of the best ways to teach adults. Asking questions is an effective way to accomplish the seven things that must happen with learners in class for disciple-making to take place.

Granted, lectures and creative learning experiences have a valid place and contribute to the learning process. For example, engaging lectures communicate information in an efficient and effective way. Good lectures, however, are rare. To be honest, most lectures are boring. God has not given many the ability to present interesting lectures. Most people, however, can be taught how to ask significant questions that lead to insightful discussions.

Creative learning experiences have their place as well. A light sprinkling of the creative can add spice to good lectures and good discussions. Caution must be observed, however, when using creative techniques. Too much creativity may come across as fun and games—something adults often resent. On the other hand, almost everyone enjoys a good conversation. That is why leading discussions is by far my favorite way to teach. I rarely speak more than a paragraph without involving the group by asking them to discuss a question. Not only are people more likely to stay interested in a topic they discuss, they are also likely to learn more in the process. This is especially true when everyone gets a chance to talk in a small group and then hears what other groups said during a report time.

Because questions are an effective means of helping people learn in class, disciple-making teachers use them liberally. In addition, disciple-making teachers ask different types of questions to achieve different results. They ask questions from most, if not all, of the following categories:

- life exposure questions,
- "What does the text say?" questions,
- "What does the text mean?" questions,
- "What was it like for them?" questions,
- "jump ball" questions,
- "Where are you now?" questions,
- application questions,
- accountability questions, and
- "How has it worked so far?" questions.

With that in mind, let's look at each type of question in a little more detail.[1]

Life Exposure Questions

I like to begin nearly every class I teach with an off-the-wall question that gets everyone mentally checked in and allows group members to learn something about each other besides their views on various biblical subjects. Some people think this is a waste of time, but I have found it to be helpful. I am careful, however, not to spend too much time on it.

I often begin class by asking people to introduce themselves and then to answer questions such as…

• What is your favorite restaurant?
• What is a favorite movie you've seen recently?
• What is your favorite television show?
• What is your favorite outdoor (indoor, spectator, participatory, summer, winter) sport?
• What is your favorite way to spend a Saturday?
• If you could live anywhere in the world, where would you live?
• If you had one life to waste, to absolutely blow on something totally outrageous, what would you waste it on?

People have answered the last question (my personal favorite) in a variety of ways, from sky diving to traveling to overdosing on drugs. This question opens the window a bit into each person's life. More important, it gets everyone talking right up front and makes it easier for people to speak up when we start discussing issues that matter even more. Finally, life exposure questions allow people to identify group members with whom they have something in common, which helps to cultivate relationships within the small group.

In addition to fun, off-the-wall questions, I also use more serious questions that in some way relate to the lesson topic. For example, if I were teaching on God's fatherhood, I might ask people to share their names and to rate, on a scale of one to ten, their relationships with their fathers as they were growing up. Or if I were teaching on wisdom and guidance, I might ask people to describe a time they felt God helped them with a decision.

These questions need to be meaningful but not so personal as to embarrass anyone. I once asked a singles group to share their names and to tell how old they were when they first kissed someone other than a family member. One girl revealed that she had never been kissed. Ouch! She was embarrassed, and so were the rest of us. Never ask questions like that.

Life exposure questions may or may not have all that much to do with the topic of the lesson. Their primary purpose is to help people check in mentally and to expose group members to one another in a friendly way. The next type of question begins to expose people to the truth.

"What Does the Text Say?" Questions

My daddy used to say, "You gotta know what the Bible says before you can know what it means." Unfortunately, all too often we want to skip over what the Bible says and move on to what it means to us, to explanation and application. Perhaps we are so familiar with the Bible that we assume everyone is. Or maybe we simply don't want to take the time to dig into the Word because it seems more interesting to go straight to principles and concepts.

> **m**y daddy used to say, "You gotta know what the Bible says before you can know what it means."

Whatever our reasons, it is safer to assume that many Christians are probably a little fuzzy on at least the details of a text and need to be reminded of them. In addition, some people don't read well, so we serve them by getting them thoroughly acquainted with what the text says. Finally, if a group is reaching out to non-Christians, there will probably be a number of people who may not know the Bible at all.

In addition to getting biblical facts out so everyone knows them, "What does the text say" questions work well to draw out quiet, shy, or introverted people. This type of question helps people become comfortable speaking up, whether in front of the entire class or within a small group. For example, sometimes I will ask a quiet person to identify one bit of information from a specific verse. Of course, I make sure to ask a question this person can successfully answer. Other times I will ask the entire class to form small groups of three to five and send them on some sort of fact-finding mission.

Let me show you what I mean. Following are several examples of "What does the text say?" questions, along with the biblical texts they relate to and different types of follow-up questions that we'll discuss in more detail later:

• In Mark 5:19, who was the demon-possessed man commanded to tell about God's work in his life? ("Jesus did not let him, but said, 'Go home to your family and tell them how much the Lord has done for you, and how he has had mercy on you.'")

Follow-up questions: Why do you think Jesus told this man to tell his family? What might be the application of this to our lives?

• How does Paul describe what God did for us in 2 Corinthians 5:21? ("God made him who had no sin to be sin for us, so that in him we might become the righteousness of God.")

Follow-up questions: Does it feel awkward to say, "God has made me to be the righteousness of God?" Why or why not? If we are God's righteousness, why do we often feel bad about ourselves? struggle with sin? What difference might it make if we truly believed this? What can we do to make sure our view of ourselves corresponds to what God says about us? (I might also talk briefly about how identity produces behavior. I believe in a rather heavy use of questions in teaching, but I'm not afraid to lecture or preach a little. Good teaching requires both good interaction around the Word and a prophetic "Thus sayeth the Lord.")

• According to Ephesians 4:11-12, what is the job description of pastors and teachers, and, by implication, what is everyone else's job description? ("It was he who gave some to be apostles, some to be prophets, and some to be evangelists, and some to be pastors and teachers, to prepare God's people for works of service, so that the body of Christ may be built up.")

Follow-up questions: What do you think these works of service include? What are some examples? What works of service have we been equipped for and performed in the last three weeks?

In some cases, you may not want to use questions to get the obvious facts out in the open. Sometimes you'll simply want to state them. For example, you might say, "Jesus told the demon-possessed man to go home and tell his family what God had done for him. What is the implication of this for our lives?" Either approach is valid. Asking "What does the text say?" questions tends to take more time, but it involves people more and establishes the Bible more firmly as your source of authority. These questions are also effective means of drawing out shy people. However, remember to limit your use of closed-ended questions so you can move on to the good stuff.

"What Does the Text Mean?" Questions

First we establish what the text says. Then we seek to establish what the text means. Some might argue that, "The Bible means what it says, and that is that." While this may be true, it is also true that sometimes it is not immediately obvious what the Bible means at all. Thoughtful and sincere students of the Bible still disagree as to the meaning of certain passages. This is part of what makes the Bible interesting. It is also what makes "What does the text mean?" questions so important.

These questions aim for a slightly deeper level of under-standing. They may involve simple definitions or explanations, or they might relate a particular biblical text to the greater context of the overall teaching of the Bible. Here are several examples:

- What do you think it means to "rejoice in the Lord always" (Philippians 4:4a)? Does this mean we must always be happy? Explain. Can we rejoice in the Lord and be sad at the same time? Explain.
- In Matthew 18:17, Jesus says we are to treat certain people as we would tax collectors. What does it mean to treat someone as a tax collector? Is Jesus telling us to treat tax collectors a certain way, or is he using this just as an example? Explain.
- In the parable of the sheep and the goats (Matthew 25:31-46), Jesus seems to separate people on the basis of their works. How can we reconcile this with the doctrine of salvation by grace through faith?
- Galatians 6:2 commands us to "carry each other's burdens." Three verses later, however, Paul states that each one of us should carry our own load. Whose load or burden are we to worry about: our own or each other's? What do you think it means to carry someone else's burden? to carry our own load?

This last question demonstrates the importance of left-brained preparation on the part of the teacher. (See page 111 for more on this.) There is actually a simple answer to it. The original Greek text of this passage uses two different words for "burden" and "load." The New International Version uses two different words to distinguish between the two, but even this does not reveal the distinction as clearly as we would like. A "burden" is a big, heavy, unbearable rock, while a "load" is a knapsack. In short, we are to carry our own knapsacks—life's daily responsibilities—but we are to help each other carry the enormous burdens that no one can bear alone.

Obviously, a teacher could simply explain this distinction rather than ask the group about it first. There will be occasions that, in the interest of time, this will be the approach to take. It is far more interesting, however, to ask the question first. People are better prepared to hear the answer after they have attempted to solve the riddle for themselves. In fact, some may even have enough knowledge or insight to explain what the passage means without your help at all. That's when you'll know that real learning is taking place.

"What Was It Like for Them?" Questions

Sometimes the world of the Bible seems far away. The events recorded in it took place on a distant continent, in a time long past, and in a different culture that spoke a different language. Knowing this, effective teachers seek to help people enter the world of the story, to see things from the perspective of the people involved. "What was it like for them?" questions are a good way to do this.

Looking beyond the text and the details of what happened into the thoughts and emotions of the people involved is especially helpful with narrative material, with the stories recorded in the Bible. Of course, we must beware of seeing things that aren't there or of projecting our own feelings onto the story's characters. But considering what biblical characters may have thought or felt often provides insight into a passage that otherwise might be missed.

STORY	QUESTIONS
The Parable of the Prodigal Son (Luke 15:11-32)	• What do you think the son was thinking as he approached his father? • How do you think the father felt when he saw his son returning? • What kind of emotions do you think the older brother experienced?
Abraham offers to sacrifice Isaac (Genesis 22:1-19)	• What do you think Abraham was thinking when he got up in the morning? • What emotions do you think Isaac felt as he was placed on the altar? • How do you think Abraham felt when he saw the ram?
Nathan confronts David for his sin (2 Samuel 12:1-14)	• What do you think was going through Nathan's mind as he prepared to talk to David? • How did he feel as he raised his hand to knock on the door? • What emotions do you think David felt when Nathan declared, "You are the man"?

Consider, for example, how "What was it like for them?" questions might draw people into the following biblical stories:

When you ask questions such as these, remember that you are not looking for a single correct answer. People often experience mixed emotions or hold various opinions about a single situation. The point is to get class members thinking about what the biblical characters probably thought and felt in their situations. If people have difficulty doing this, you might suggest a few possible responses. For example, you might ask, "Do you think David felt defensive or convicted when Nathan confronted him?" In fact, he may have felt both, which makes this a good "jump ball" question, the topic of our next section.

Before we move on, however, let's take a moment to review. Thus far we have discussed four types of questions. How well can you remember which ones we covered?

The rest of the discussion will address five other kinds of questions that can involve people in life-changing discussions about God:

- "jump ball" questions,
- "Where are you now?" questions,
- application questions,
- accountability questions, and
- "How has it worked so far?" questions.

"Jump Ball" Questions

When the class gets into the heart of a lesson, I like to toss out a "jump ball" question. Good "jump ball" questions can legitimately go either way. If a "jump ball" question is phrased well, some people will answer it one way, while others will take the opposite view. With the right "jump ball" questions, the teacher can often sit back and let group members wrestle with the issue for a while.

> What we want to create is a discussion in which the teacher is a player—perhaps the leading player, but still just a player.

What we want to create is a discussion in which the teacher is a player—perhaps the leading player, but still just a player. These type of questions differ significantly from those that simply create a dialogue between the teacher and the learner. "Jump ball" questions encourage learners to interact with each other.

Here is an example of a "jump ball" question I have had success with in the past. If you teach a group, you might want to use this one the next time you are together and see where it goes:

- Is Christianity easy or hard?

In my opinion, this question can be answered yes or no. Experience will lead most people to think that Christianity is difficult, and the Bible does contain evidence in support of this view (Ephesians 6:10-12; Philippians 3:12-14; Hebrews 12:1-4). But Jesus also said that his yoke is easy and his burden light (Matthew 11:30). That leads me to conclude that Christianity, like dancing, is either easy or impossible. Skilled dancers make dancing look easy. But this fluidity requires discipline and hard work.

Christianity ought to look easy. There ought to be a grace, a poise, and a joy in it that makes it easy. Christianity is at its best when we enjoy God most. Still, God demands everything from us. We must deny ourselves, take up our crosses, and follow Jesus. We must give up everything to be Christ's disciples. In one way Christianity is easy, and in another way it is hard. That is why this is a good "jump ball" question.

Sometimes the trajectory of a "jump ball" question will need to be altered slightly, either because you miscalculated the release or because everyone in the group agrees on the answer. If this happens, you simply need to take the other side.

For example, if everyone agrees that Christianity is hard, ask, "What about Matthew 11:30, which says that Jesus' yoke is easy and his burden light? What is the answer according to that verse?" If, on the other hand, everyone states that Christianity is easy, ask, "Is it *always* easy for you?"

Sometimes I alter the trajectory of a "jump ball" question simply to push the discussion a little further or in a different direction. For example, I asked the following question of two different groups and got completely different reactions. So I had to alter the trajectory of the question in order to create the discussion. To launch the jump ball, I told a story:

> I was talking with someone the other day, and at a certain point in the conversation I said, "It sounds as though you're saying that if a sinner came to God and asked for help to quit sinning, God might tell that person no." "That's exactly what I am saying," he replied. Reflect on that for a minute. Do you think it's true?

Interestingly enough, every member of the first group agreed that sometimes God would decline that prayer request. The second group, however, immediately replied, "God would never say that. He would always come to the aid of a sinner who asked for it." In both cases, I presented the opposite view in order to create a dialogue. Then, after some discussion, I pushed a little further: "What about with regard to knowing God—could it be that someone would come to God and ask to know him better, and God would say no?"

The point of the first question was to open people to the idea that it is possible to ask God for help overcoming sin and have the wrong motives. Maybe sin has damaged an addict's life, and this person simply wants God to do what therapy or a twelve-step program could not do. In this case, someone may not really be interested in God, and God might say no.

With that established, I altered the trajectory of the discussion so people would learn that it is possible to ask to know God better and to have wrong motives in doing so. The question asked of Job is also asked of everyone else, "Does Job fear God for nothing?" (Job 1:9). Will you? Will I? Or do we want to know God for what we will get out of it? God is more than a quick-fix or a new high. God wants us to enjoy our relationship with him, but he wants us to approach him with pure motives.

During the dialogue prompted by the "jump ball" question, these tensions should become clear. Within the tensions of the discussion, a clearer picture of the truth generally emerges. Truth is often the tension between two seemingly opposite truths or viewpoints. The skillful disciple-making teacher realizes this and leads people into life-changing dialogues centered around God's Word.

My life has been permanently altered by stimulating, informed conversations. "Jump ball" questions create such conversations. The test of a "jump ball" question is how long it keeps the group talking. If people are still talking about it at the potluck dinner after church, it is a *good* question. If people's lives are different because they engaged their minds with this question, it is a really *great* "jump ball" question.

"Where Are You Now?" Questions

Learning requires us to see the gap between where we are now and where God would have us to be. Life-change takes place when we see that gap and decide, by God's grace, to repent of being where we are now and to strive to move where God would have us to be. "Where are you now?" questions help people see this gap. These questions ask people to identify where they are now with relation to the issue being discussed.

In most cases, this is best done indirectly. People tend to become defensive if we ask them "Where are you now?" questions directly. It is far better to ask, "How would you describe the average Christian: totally committed to God, totally cold toward God, or somewhere in between?" After people respond, you might ask more directly, "And how would you describe yourself?"

Indirect questions can be answered out loud. Direct questions, on the other hand, should be asked rhetorically, permitting people to answer silently. Nevertheless, you need to ask direct questions. The Bible directs us to "examine" or to "test" ourselves (2 Corinthians 13:5). That is what these questions seek to do.

Sometimes it is helpful to hand out pencils and paper and to ask people to answer the direct "Where are you now?" question on paper. Some people think better when they write things out, and this approach encourages everyone to be involved. For example, you might ask people to draw line graphs tracing the progress of their spiritual lives. The top of each graph represents a strong spiritual life, while the bottom of the graph indicates distance from God. This approach also enables people to evaluate themselves honestly without compromising their privacy.

If you want people to see the gap between where they are now and where God wants them to be, you need to ask "Where are you now?" questions. If you want people to answer these questions honestly, you must respect their privacy.

Application Questions

Application is the goal of disciple-making teaching. As Howard Hendricks states, "We are not out to make smarter sinners, but saints." Application is not something we tack on to the end of a good discussion. It is the point of the discussion. In good teaching, all roads lead to application. Every question, discussion, example, verse, story, illustration, activity, or lecture—all of them lead to application.

Application questions are fairly straightforward, but some are better than others. For example, if you ask, "How can we apply this truth to our lives?" you need to encourage people to be specific. Application is effective to the degree that it is spe-cific. You might also ask, "Specifically, *how* do we go about enjoying God?" Another good question is, "What advice would you give to a friend who did not see himself or herself as God's righteousness, as 2 Corinthians 5:21 states?" People are often better at giving advice to a friend than they are at telling exactly how they would do something. Other helpful application questions might include…

• What specific steps could we take to make this a reality in our day-to-day lives?

• What is one thing you could do for your spouse this week that would demonstrate a servant's heart? Name something you were not already planning to do.

The key to good application questions is their specificity. Resist the temptation to be too grandiose. Christians love to talk about how we need to serve God and forsake the world and so on. All of this is true, of course, but what specifically are we going to do to serve God? How do we forsake the world? What television programs will we quit watching? What books are we going to read, and what books are we going to stop reading? Talk about specific things people can do this week and every week that follows.

People forget most of what they hear. They even forget a good deal of what they see and talk about (though retention with these is better than with simply hearing something). But people remember most of what they do. If you can prompt group members to do one small thing in application of the truth they learned, you will greatly increase their chances of remembering that truth. There is a good chance their lives will be permanently altered if they do something—anything—as a result of the lesson.

The other side of the application issue is that there is much more to being a disciple than simply "doing." Discipleship also involves knowing, believing, and feeling. It is about attitude. If people know and believe that God is all-knowing, all-powerful, unchanging, holy, transcendent, loving, kind, and merciful, they will be on their way to living the disciple's life. These beliefs will alter their attitudes and, in turn, their lives.

In fact, one could argue that it is impossible for someone truly to be a growing, maturing disciple unless most of his or her concepts about God are accurate. Being thoroughly impressed with God's holiness is important. Doing can come later. People first need to understand something about God. So teachers need to relax and not push only for "doing-based" applications. Application also involves repenting of false beliefs and embracing truth. In sum, application often starts with knowing and believing, then progresses to feeling, and concludes with doing.

Let me show you what I mean by asking a "jump ball" question: Is loving God a decision, an emotion, or an action?

One might argue that loving God is primarily an action. However, discipleship involves much more than being good. There is far more to the Christian life than simply doing the right thing. The Pharisees did that, and Jesus reserved his most potent rebukes for them. We must be ever vigilant against the sin of pharisaism that defines righteousness merely (or pri-marily) in terms of externals.

Likewise, although disciple-making teachers need to help people think the right things—teach them that loving God is the right thing to do—this is clearly not enough. The Bible also commands us to feel the right things. "Never be lacking in zeal" (Romans 12:11a) is a command to feel fervently about God. "Rejoice in the Lord always" (Philippians 4:4a) is a command to enjoy God. The God of the Bible is a God of deep emotions, and we are to be like him. We are to feel love for him—a love based in truth and expressed in action. In short, if you want to make disciples, you must challenge people to think, feel, and do the right things.

Perhaps the one word that best sums up the focus of application is "attitude." Our attitude is influenced by our beliefs, shapes our emotions, and affects our behavior. The three realms of application are beliefs, emotions, and behavior. Attitude encompasses all three.

Time for a review. Let me hold you accountable for what you have learned thus far. How many types of questions can you remember?

Accountability Questions

Closed, discipleship groups have an inherent advantage over open, evangelistic groups with regard to accountability. In a closed group, a teacher can build discipleship momentum because people know they will be held accountable every session for the previous lesson's application goals. If you are teaching about the discipline of regular Bible reading, you can hold the group accountable for reading their Bibles. This is an enormous help in the disciple-making process. For this reason, every church should provide at least some closed, discipleship groups.

However, this disciple-making comes with a price. It is difficult to maintain this level of accountability and an inviting, including atmosphere at the same time. That's why churches also need open, evangelistic groups. Open groups can take people at any level of spiritual maturity and move them along the disciple-making process…up to a point. Closed, accountability groups can move people to a higher level than open groups, but they have a limited usefulness in offering an inviting, including community.

In open groups, meaningful needs to be short-term. If group members commit to pray for each other this week, I need to ask them about it the next. If I challenge the group to perform one random act of love one week, I need to hold them accountable for it the next. People who are new to the group will not feel as though they've walked in on the middle of something. They will realize that this was an application of last week's lesson, and if they come next week, they will be right up to speed.

With applications that involve developing the right feelings, you may need to do more than simply ask people whether they followed through with their commitments. For example, if a particular lesson dealt with the idea that we are to enjoy God (Psalm 37:4; Philippians 3:1; 4:4), I might ask the next week, "Did anyone have any moments this week when you enjoyed God? Tell us about it." Or if I taught a lesson on the fatherhood of God, I might ask the following week, "Did you have a chance to think about God as Father? How have your feelings toward God changed this week?"

One final note about accountability: If you promise to keep people accountable, don't break your promise. I have seen too many teachers break their word to the detriment of the group. Suppose a teacher challenges the group, "Who will read through the book of Philippians every day this week? I am going to hold you accountable." You are motivated to do this, so you diligently take time each day to read the four chapters that make up Philippians. But when you walk into class feeling good that you kept your commitment, the teacher forgets all about the previous week's commitment. How would you feel? Don't make the people in your class feel that way.

> If you promise to keep people accountable, don't break your promise.

"How Has It Worked So Far?" Questions

More people are persuaded by the group than they are by the naked truth. That is why we facetiously ask our kids, "If all your friends jumped in the fire, would you jump in, too?" The ironic reality that we seldom think about is that the answer to this question is "yes" more often than we know.

Consider Jonestown, for example. I know a man who was among the first group of people to go to Guyana to investigate what had happened. He explained why early estimates of the number of dead were so low (about three hundred versus the actual number of about nine hundred). The investigators knew about how many people lived in the commune, yet they didn't see that many bodies. So they assumed hundreds of people had fled into the jungle. That makes sense, because we think that is what we would do if someone asked us to drink cyanide-laced Kool-Aid. We forget about the pull of the crowd. What the team didn't realize was that people drank the cyanide and then lay down to die on those who were already dead, so that dead bodies were stacked three, four, and five deep. There is incredible power in the influence of a group, whether for evil or for good.

> More people are persuaded by the group than they are by the naked truth.

We often think of peer pressure as a teenage issue. It isn't. Peer pressure affects everyone. So teachers should capitalize on this fact in the disciple-making process. Consider this: Every Sunday school class and adult Bible study contains a wide variety of people with different levels of spiritual maturity. So instead of simply telling people, for example, that they ought to have a quiet time, why not allow three or four group members to share their personal stories about having a quiet time? Why not invite members of the group to answer questions such as...

- What does it mean to them?
- What specifically do they do?
- How did they get started?
- Why do they have a quiet time? and
- What are the rewards?

These personal stories will be far more compelling than your persuasive words. Most people are persuaded by their friends. They do what they see their friends doing. So with nearly every area of application, you should ask people who are already living out that truth to tell the rest of the group about it.

For example, if you are teaching on making peace with your past, ask, "Who can tell a story of coming to grips with some painful issues in your past and finding healing for them?" If the lesson is on Scripture memory, you could ask, "Who has experienced success in memorizing God's Word? What helped you to be successful?" If you are teaching on sharing one's faith, ask, "Has anyone had a chance to share his or her faith in the past few months?" The answers to these questions will have a powerful effect on your group.

On the other hand, sometimes testimonies are counterproductive, with disastrous results. Suppose group members were holding each other accountable for having a daily quiet time. When, however, the leader asks how the group did this week, someone pipes up, "I didn't do so well—not once this week." Another person adds, "Yeah, I didn't do any better." Someone else remarks, "I read my Bible one day, but I didn't get much out of it." Be careful that "testimony time" doesn't degenerate into a "feeling good about failure" session in which group members assuage each other's guilt for not living the disciple's life.

Finally, make sure that this does not turn into a bragging session for the spiritually pompous. Some people enjoy telling how well they are doing altogether too much. They enjoy the oohs and the aahs, the admiration of the group. Some are constantly seeking an audience before whom they can show off. This is not the place for that.

Robert B. Cialdini has done significant research on the psychology of influence. He identifies several key factors that relate to influence. Perhaps the most important is social proof.[2] In short, Cialdini concludes that we do as we see being done. The power of the pack over us is great. We can take advantage of this in the disciple-making process by allowing people to tell others "how it has worked so far," to share stories of how God is working in and changing their lives.

Before we conclude with an example of how these different types of questions might work in a single lesson, I'd like you to review what you have learned so far. See if you can recall the nine kinds of questions disciple-making teachers can use to teach a group.

Did you remember them all? If not, focus on those that you forgot as you read this concluding example. Imagine that you are teaching a group of Sunday school teachers and small-group leaders. Your goal is to help them learn and apply the principles revealed in the example of Apollos (Acts 18:24-26). Here are some questions you might use.

Life Exposure Question

- What is one thing you have going for you as a teacher?

"What Does the Text Say?" Questions

- As you read Acts 18:24-26, what do you notice that Apollos had going for him as a teacher?
- Tell me about an "Apollos" you have known, a teacher who spoke with fervency and accuracy and who was a lifelong learner. How did this teacher influence your life?

"What Does the Text Mean?" Questions

- According to verse 24, Apollos had a "thorough" knowledge of the Scriptures. What does this mean? How thorough is thorough? How well must you know the Bible in order to teach effectively?
- Apollos was from Alexandria. What can you tell me about this city? Does this affect your view of Apollos at all?

"What Was It Like for Them?" Questions

- How does great teaching affect you? How does it feel when you sit in the class of a really good teacher?
- How do you think Apollos' "class" felt as they listened to him teach?
- How do you think Apollos felt when Aquila and Priscilla began explaining to him "the way of God more accurately"? Do you think he was threatened, thrilled, or something else?

"Jump Ball" Question

- Which do you think is more important in teaching: accuracy or fervency? Explain your answer.

"Where Are You Now?" Questions

- How would you rate the accuracy of the average teacher in the average class in the average church?
- How would you evaluate the teachers you have learned from in terms of their fervency?
- Without answering out loud, how would you say you are doing in terms of presenting the truth with accuracy?
- On a scale of one to ten, how would you evaluate your "fervency factor"? Again, you don't need to answer out loud.

Application Questions

- Why do you think accuracy in teaching is important? Why do you think fervency is important?
- In addition to fervency and accuracy, what does it take to make a great teacher?
- Suppose a teacher told you, "I struggle with teaching with as much enthusiasm as I need. How can I become someone who teaches with great fervor?" What would you tell that person?
- Are you ever excited while preparing a lesson but less so when it comes time to teach? How can you address this problem?
- What can you do to make sure that your teaching is as accurate as possible?

Accountability Question

- What specifically have you done to improve your teaching in the past few weeks?

"How Has It Worked So Far?" Question

- What have been the results of these improvements?

Asking questions is perhaps the most effective means of making disciples, but it's not the only method. Another effective strategy is the use of the repeated phrase, the subject of our next discussion.

The Repeated Phrase

Whether used in sermons or in small groups, the repeated phrase is one of the most effective ways to communicate a central idea. If you want to drive home a key point, make liberal use of the repeated phrase. Consider, for example, how the repeated phrase contributes to one of the most powerful speeches ever crafted. Read through a portion of this stirring piece, and circle every occurrence of the phrase, "I have a dream."

> If you want to drive home a key point, make liberal use of the repeated phrase.

> I say to you today, my friends, that in spite of the difficulties and frustrations of the moment, I still have a dream. It is a dream deeply rooted in the American dream.
> I have a dream that one day this nation will rise up and live out the true meaning of its creed: 'We hold these truths to be self-evident: that all men are created equal.'
> I have a dream that one day on the red hills of Georgia the sons of former slaves and the sons of former slaveowners will be able to sit down together at a table of brotherhood.
> I have a dream that one day even the state of Mississippi, a desert state, sweltering with the heat of injustice and oppression, will be transformed into an oasis of freedom and justice.
> I have a dream that my four children will one day live in a nation where they will not be judged by the color of their skin but by the content of their character.
> I have a dream today.
> I have a dream that one day the state of Alabama, whose governor's lips are presently dripping with the words of interposition and nullification, will be transformed into a situation where little black boys and black girls will be able to join hands with little white boys and white girls and walk together as sisters and brothers.
> I have a dream today.
> I have a dream that one day every valley shall be exalted, every hill and mountain shall be made low, the rough places will be made plain, and the crooked places will be made straight, and the glory of the Lord shall be revealed, and all flesh shall see it together.[3]

Within the 288 words that make up the heart of one of the most powerful and memorable speeches that has ever been delivered, the exact phrase "I have a dream" occurs eight times. The words "I have a dream" constitute 11 percent of this section of the speech. Four words repeated eight times within one short segment. We might be tempted to think that this would become repetitious, boring, and monotonous…but it doesn't. This speech is powerful and memorable because of the repeated phrase, not in spite of it.

Disciple-making teachers need to understand the power of the repeated phrase. Here is yet another example, from the introduction of the same speech. I suspect that you will have little difficulty finding the repeated phrase.

> Five score years ago, a great American, in whose symbolic shadow we stand signed the Emancipation Proclamation. This momentous decree came as a great beacon light of hope to millions of Negro slaves who had been seared in the flames of withering injustice. It came as a joyous daybreak to end the long night of captivity.
>
> But one hundred years later, we must face the tragic fact that the Negro is still not free. One hundred years later, the life of the Negro is still sadly crippled by the manacles of segregation and the chains of discrimination. One hundred years later, the Negro lives on a lonely island of poverty in the midst of a vast ocean of material prosperity. One hundred years later, the Negro is still languishing in the corners of American
> society and finds himself an exile in his own land. So we have come here today to dramatize an appalling condition.

Do you feel the cadence and drama that this repeated phrase gives to the speech? The repeated phrase gives the speech clarity, focus, direction, and power.

The repeated phrase can also be used in a small-group setting, with almost any topic. If, for example, you are teaching enjoying God, you might ask some of the following questions, using the phrase "enjoy God" repeatedly.

- Why are we commanded to "rejoice in the Lord" and to "delight [ourselves] in the Lord" (Philippians 3:1; Psalm 37:4)? Why do you think God wants us to enjoy him?
- Who have you known whom you would describe as someone who enjoyed God?
- What do you think it means in real-life terms to enjoy God?
- What difference would enjoying God make in our daily lives?
- What do you think we can do to develop real enjoyment of God?

In the course of this discussion, the phrase "enjoying God" would be repeated over and over, both by the teacher and by the members of the group. When the group walked out the door, the phrase "enjoying God" would be ringing in their ears. People would continue to ask themselves these questions about what it means to enjoy God and how they can enjoy God.

This book offers another example of a repeated phrase. Throughout this book, I have written about the goal of becoming a disciple-making teacher. Not only do I discuss this idea from various angles, I repeat the actual phrase, "disciple-making teacher" over and over again. If you look carefully, you will also discover a repeated phrase in this discussion. This repeated phrase is used over and over so that you will remember the importance of using repeated phrases. The repeated phrase is one of the most effective ways to convey a central truth or point. Use the repeated phrase repeatedly.

Stuff You Can Touch and Feel

"As the Pharisees scorned her, people began running through the crowd handing out stones." As I say this, ten young people grab the bags of rocks from under their chairs and begin passing them out. "Take these, you'll need them," they bark. Everyone takes a stone. I continue to speak. "Imagine what it felt like that day to hold a stone in your hand, knowing this stone would be one of the stones used to execute this woman, this adulteress. Hold the rock in your hand. Feel its texture. What are you thinking as you lift that rock to throw it at her? Are you thinking, 'She's guilty; she deserves to die! We have our law. Rules are rules.'

"Perhaps you are one of her ex-husbands. Perhaps she cheated on you, and you want to kill her. You can hardly wait to throw that rock. You're convinced that she is getting what she deserves. You feel good about justice being served.

"Or perhaps you are admitting to yourself that you also are guilty. You have done what this adulteress did, in thought if not in deed. You also deserve to die. You wish someone would have pity on you. You wonder, 'Is there any way to satisfy the demands of the law without killing her, without killing me?'

"Now I want you to set down your stone. And as you do, I want you to set down the desire within you to condemn. I ask you to embrace the belief that the demands of the law were satisfied at the cross of Christ. I ask you to set down a heart of condemnation and to embrace a heart of grace. Who are you angry at? Who do you want to condemn? Who has sinned against you so horribly that you are tempted to think that that sin exceeds the limit of Christ's sacrifice on the cross? I ask you to forgive that person. I ask you to set down, not only that stone, but also the right to condemn.

"You see, either Christ's death on the cross was sufficient to pay for sin—all sin—or it wasn't. If it didn't pay for every sin, then it wasn't sufficient to take care of our sin, and we are all in deep trouble. If the cross was sufficient, it was sufficient to cover sins by you and against you.

"So set down that stone. Go ahead, set it down—and with it, set down a heart of anger. Set down your unforgiving, condemning heart, and embrace a heart of love, mercy, acceptance, and grace.

"The gospel is all about grace—grace for me and grace for you, grace for those who have sinned against me and grace for those who have sinned against you. The gospel is all about grace, so set down your stony heart and embrace a heart of grace."

Giving people stuff to touch and feel, to hold and smell can create a powerful learning experience that mere words can never match. We are physical and spiritual beings, and our bodies affect our spirits just as our spirits affect our bodies. Our spirits are affected when we see, touch, feel, and smell objects. Learning increases when we engage our bodies and our emotions and not just our minds.[4]

Jesus used objects people could touch and feel all the time. Many of his miracles were, in fact, "acted-out parables." Jesus' calming of the storm wasn't just about water and boats, was it? Class was in session. Jesus was teaching about the storms of life, about how he is so relaxed during the storms that he can sleep, and about how he can make a stormy sea as calm as glass merely by speaking the word. It wasn't simply a miracle; it was an acted-out parable. Stuff you could touch and feel and see and hold, a concrete demonstration of an eternal truth. The disciples never forgot it.

Jesus also touched the lepers when he healed them. This wouldn't seem a big deal to people who experience human touch on a regular basis. Being touched is like breathing air: when you have enough, you don't think too much about it. But these lepers were starving for human touch. So Jesus used his miraculous powers to heal their leprosy and the power of human touch to heal their souls.

Jesus also promised his disciples that if they would follow him, he would teach them to fish for people. One of the final days of class went as follows (John 21:1-14). Jesus had died and the disciples had gone back to the only thing they knew: fishing. The only problem was that they had apparently lost their touch after three years of following Jesus. These professional fishermen were an utter failure at the one thing they knew how to do in life. They worked all night and caught nothing. Then the resurrected Jesus advised them to let down their nets on the right side of the boat. They obeyed and caught so many fish that they didn't know what to do with them. Class was in session. The lesson was: Follow me, and you will do just fine.

I wonder if the disciples thought about this when Jesus told them to make disciples of all nations. After all, their first move was to seclude themselves in an upper room and pray—hardly a strategy for gathering a crowd. But then God's Spirit filled them with the power to declare the gospel, and three thousand people came to believe in Jesus. I wonder if Peter thought about those fish.

When Jesus told the disciples, "Look at the fields!" I believe he pointed to actual fields (John 4:35). When Jesus declared, "Let the little children come to me," I suspect that his hand rested on the shoulder of a dark-haired child (Mark 10:14). Likewise, when Jesus taught a lesson about condemnation and forgiveness, the people set down actual stones that they were prepared to throw.

Effective disciple-making teachers make use of stuff that people can touch and hold and smell and feel. They bring rocks to class and pass them around. They have people draw and make lists. They hold up lampshades when they teach on being the light of the world. They pass out packets of salt and ask, "What needs to happen for this salt to do anyone any good?"

Whenever you teach, ask yourself if there is any physical object or experience you can use to enhance the teaching of the lesson. You don't have to do this every time you meet. In fact, if you do, the creativity itself will become routine and boring. The unusual nature of the experience is what makes this approach effective. Still, you should be giving people stuff to touch and experiences to feel on a regular basis. Doing so will make your teaching more effective and your group members' learning more memorable.

> **W**hen Jesus told the disciples, "Look at the fields!" I believe he pointed to actual fields (John 4:35).

Video

Videos offer us the unprecedented opportunity to expose people to some of the finest teachers on planet Earth. What other generation could have done this? So it isn't too smart to completely ignore this resource. Videos have a place in the classrooms of disciple-making teachers.

I love good video teaching, but not every week and not the entire hour. People still need time to engage in discussion and to complete active learning experiences. This is why full-hour videos frustrate me: They leave no time for discussion. So I generally stop the video in the middle and discuss it anyway. Or sometimes I stop the video several times and have people discuss related questions for five or ten minutes. My advice is to use videos in class but not to let them dominate.

To use videos as a launch pad for discussion and active learning, give people an assignment before you start the tape. Give everyone a piece of paper and a pencil, explain what the video is about, then challenge each person to write down one thing he or she learns from the video. Tell people you will be asking them to share what they discover. People listen to the entire tape differently when they know they will have to talk about what they learn. They cannot be passive observers; they must become active learners. In addition, as each person shares, others are reminded of the key points of the video. People may resist, but gently push them to take notes and to be prepared to share.

A curious dynamic (and benefit) of videos is that they offer one of the few times it seems acceptable to disagree with the speaker. If you disagree with your own pastor, you may sound like a heretic or a complainer. People often hesitate to disagree with a Sunday school teacher or a small-group leader for the same reason. But people can disagree with a video teacher without seeming to be troublemakers. In fact, they often seem insightful because the disagreement helps to sharpen everyone's understanding.

> a curious dynamic (and benefit) of videos is that they offer one of the few times it seems acceptable to disagree with the speaker.

Another advantage of video is that it gives the teacher a break from teaching. Every teacher has more than enough to do: shepherd the group, cultivate group life, and so on. By periodically taking a break from teaching, the teacher can devote his or her efforts to the other tasks needed to grow and to nurture a class.

The disadvantage of video is obvious: It is strictly passive, often with no discussion, no interaction, and no activity. It is unlikely that we can make disciples without small-group discussions, active learning experiences, and times for personal application. Merely watching television will not get the job done. People need to process how the information applies to their lives. Again, this can be an especially serious problem with videos that take up the entire class time. It is far better to use a video for twenty minutes and then give people ample time to discuss, experience, and apply what they learned.

Video teaching will never replace live teaching in the disciple-making process. Videos can, however, supplement and augment what the teacher does. Use them judiciously.

Review, Review, Review

One reason no one learns much of anything at church is that we believe teaching is primarily telling and that telling once is enough. This is a false belief. We need to reject it. If you don't believe me, I dare you to walk into class next week and ask your group, "What did you do about last week's lesson?" I guarantee that the vast majority in the group will not even remember last week's lesson, much less have done anything about it. That is why we must review, review, review.

Take a hint from advertising. Do advertisers believe they can tell us something once and permanently change our spending patterns? Not on your life. That is why you see the same commercials over and over, year after year. Disciple-making teachers need to learn from their example.

Likewise, do parents think they can tell their kids something one time and never tell them again? If telling only once works for you, please write a book on parenting. I want to know your secret! I have to tell my kids something over and over and over again.

> One reason no one learns much of anything at church is that we believe teaching is primarily telling and that telling once is enough.

If your ego can handle it, try what I did several weeks ago. I was leading a small group that had just spent three months studying J. I. Packer's classic work, Knowing God. I wanted to review a bit, so I asked, "Tell me one thing that has impressed you this last three months—either from reading the book itself, from our discussions, or from any other source. What have you learned about knowing God recently?" Their silence was not golden. I resolved that day to do a better job of review. Granted, people probably learned some truths—even though they could not remember specifically what they were—and moved forward in the disciple-making process. Still, I wanted to do better.

I contrast that with a sermon series I delivered on the book of Nehemiah. I adopted the perspective that Nehemiah was a success and that we can become successes by following his example. To help organize my main points, I summarized the five "big ideas" of the series under five A-words:
- Ask in prayer,
- Aim,
- Act,
- Assess, and
- Adjust.

Then I preached one or more sermons on each point, illustrating what each point meant from the life of Nehemiah. Nearly every week I asked the congregation to review the main points. By the time the series was done I would step to the pulpit, hold up one finger, and ask, "What does the first A stand for?" A loud response would come back at me, "Ask in prayer." "Second A?" "Aim." And so on all the way through the list. I was amazed at how well people remembered the main points of the series when I took the time to review it with them. Of course, there is far more to disciple-making than listing a series of words, but this is a good place to begin. Comprehension precedes application.

I had a similar experience when I used the Bold Love video series with another small group. The study did not lend itself to listing five points in an acrostic, but I did ask the group nearly every week to rehearse the main ideas covered up to that point. By the end of the course I was asking even shy individuals to summarize the series in one paragraph, and they could do it. Obviously, disciple-making extends far beyond this, but it does include teaching people things to remember.

To be honest, I am not quite sure why we hesitate to do this, why we think that review is unnecessary. Perhaps…

• we believe people will get it the first time.

• we're worried that people will be bored with review.

• we are so excited about this week's lesson that we don't want to spend time talking about last week's.

• we really don't understand the larger picture ourselves, and it is easier simply to study each tree as we pass by than it is to climb to a high place where we can see the entire forest.

• we can't remember ourselves what we taught last week. (Now, there's a thought!)

• we are afraid of what we will find out if we ask people what they have learned thus far. (Ouch!)

Disciple-making teachers are not overly worried about any of these possibilities. They regularly spend time reviewing what has been taught to make sure that it has actually been learned. They recognize that this isn't a test of class members, though some may perceive it that way. If anything, it is a test of the teacher. It is the teacher's job to teach. If people aren't learning, it is the teacher's job to do something about it. Review closes the feedback loop so the teacher can find out if people really did hear and understand.

> Perhaps we can't remember ourselves what we taught last week.

Of course, the best review does not have to do with review of content; it has to do with holding people accountable for application. Ask the group regularly,

"What difference is this making in your life? Are you finding ways to put these truths to practice?"

Preview is also an effective means of helping people remember truth over the long term. Of course, this assumes that you as a teacher know where you are headed beyond the next lesson. You don't have to know the details, but you should be able to say, for example, "In the next few weeks we will be discussing six principles of biblical money management. Let's preview what they are…" Preview and review help people learn and retain more over the long haul.

Let me show you what I mean. In the discussion on "Asking Good Questions," I previewed the nine different types of questions at the beginning of the discussion, asked you to review the types we had discussed several times during the discussion, previewed the remaining types after each review, and asked you to name all nine types at the end of the discussion. My question is: How well would you have remembered the different types of questions if I had simply discussed them one after another, with no preview and review? My guess is that you wouldn't have remembered as many as you did by the end of the discussion. Moreover, I suspect that if you reviewed the different types of questions by reciting them out loud several times a week, you could remember them easily within a very short time. Learning is easy when we review. It is nearly impossible when we do not. So give your group the same advantage that I gave you.

Let's try another one. This is the heart and soul of this book, so I hope you take this seriously. It will make you a better teacher if you do. I have said that four things must happen for disciple-making to take place. I have mentioned three to this point, but how well have you learned them? To find out, summarize what you remember about each section. If you get stumped, go ahead and look back. But let yourself struggle a bit. On the next page, I will give you my summaries.

- **The learner outside of class: a certain kind of life**

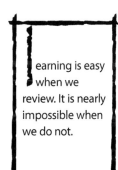

earning is easy when we review. It is nearly impossible when we do not.

- **The learner in class: a certain kind of learning**

- **The teacher in class: a certain kind of presentation**

- **The teacher out of class: a certain kind of preparation**
  (Still to come.)

Review Answers

- **The learner outside of class: a certain kind of life**
  D isciplined in daily walk with God
  I ntimate friendships
  S elf-esteem
  C orporate worship
  I ntimate family life
  P assion for God
  L ay ministry
  E vangelistic interest
  S acrificial giving

- **The learner in class: a certain kind of learning**
  After addressing barriers to learning, we surveyed the learning
  process. The learning process includes getting people interested,
  turning truth into truth that matters, showing how that truth relates
  to their Monday mornings, pointing out the gap between where
  they are and where they should be, presenting the benefits of
  obedience and the drawbacks of disobedience, leading people to
  make commitments to change, and holding people accountable for
  their commitments.

- **The teacher in class: a certain kind of presentation**

Thus far we have discussed nine types of questions that involve people in the lesson, the use of the repeated phrase, experiential learning, video, and review.

- **The teacher outside of class: a certain kind of preparation** (Still to come.)

I hope you see in this review a number of ideas that you may have thought were helpful when you read them but that you had forgotten about since then. I hope this will be a living demonstration of the importance of review, both for you and for the people in your group.

Giving Everyone a Chance to Talk

Presenting a certain kind of lesson involves far more than using helpful teaching methods such as questions, the repeated phrase, learning experiences, video, and review. It also means maintaining a certain kind of learning environment, an environment in which each person is involved as much as possible.

Unfortunately, it only takes one person to single-handedly destroy that learning environment. All the prayer, study, and preparation that went into the lesson can be ruined by one person who talks too much. Someone who dominates discussions frustrates teachers who want to teach and learners who came to learn. Here is what you can do to rein in an overly talkative person.

One way to keep overtalkers from dominating a discussion is to form discussion groups of three to five people each. This way, more people will be involved. The overtalker may still dominate his or her group, but the other groups will get along nicely and learn more. These small groups need not last the entire hour; sometimes five to ten minutes is enough. Sometimes you will give each group a different assignment, while other times you can ask several groups to investigate the same question. Whatever the case, give each group something to discover and something to discuss.

When the small groups finish their assignments, you will want to have them report what they discovered to the rest of the class. When they do, you might ask the overtalker to report for his or her group. This may run counter to your intuition, since you want this person to talk less and everyone else to talk more, but there is a good reason for doing so. It may be that the overtalker has never been called on to speak, probably because he or she has already always been talking. This person may have a need to be heard, and you might be meeting that need by calling on him or her to speak.

If this need is filled, this person might be satisfied and tend to talk less. Notice that I said "might." There are no guarantees, but it's worth a try.

If the problem is mild but persistent, you might try the indirect appeal. That is, begin each class session with a statement of lesson goals. For example, you might say, "My goal for this class is to involve everyone in the discussion. Does everyone agree that this is a good goal? OK, then I want to ask for your help. Some of you need to get really brave and dive in a little more often, while some of you need to back off until everyone has had a chance to talk. I'm not trying to limit discussion. Quite the contrary, I am trying to get everyone talking. So if we get into the discussion, you have shared several times, and you notice some of the rest have not shared as much, I want to ask you to wait until they do. Fair enough?"

Encourage everyone to nod and agree. If the problem persists, you can probably remind everyone about the goal only once more during class. After this, you usually need to move on to the "private-and-polite" appeal.

The private-and-polite appeal has the same goal and works in much the same way as the indirect appeal. But because it is private, it tends to be more direct and, therefore, more effective. The key is to approach this as an appeal to a common goal (good group discussion), not as a scolding, which never really works. In some ways, you make a hero out of the overtalker by enlisting him or her to help you. For example, you might say, "Paul, have you noticed that I can't seem to get everyone in the class talking? It is really frustrating for me as a teacher. I was wondering if you could help me? Here is what I have in mind. I know you know the answer to a lot of the questions I ask. Oftentimes, you answer exactly right as soon as I ask a question. While this gets us the right answer right away, I would still like to see if I could get some of the quiet people talking. What would you think about helping me out by not answering so quickly? Let's see if we can get everyone involved."

When the private-and-polite appeal doesn't work, it's time to be more direct. The needs of the many outweigh the needs of the few. It is better to hurt one person's feelings, if that is what it takes, than to let that person ruin the entire lesson for everyone else. There is a lot riding on this, so you'll need to be courageous. If it comes down to it, you should be ready to say something like, "Joe, can I shoot straight with you? You are talking about twice as much as anyone else in the group. While you have some good things to say, others won't talk when you talk so much. I need to ask you to back off a bit. How about if you make sure that you don't talk a second time until everyone else has talked at least once. I really need you to do this for the group. Can you do that for me?"

Effectively dealing with overly talkative people is easier when we understand what drives them. I can think of at least two things. Some are simply extroverts. They are fun-loving, enjoy-talking, happy people. They are the easiest to deal with. Sometimes we can even make a joke out of the problem with these people: "Come on, Mary, let someone else have a chance."

Other overtalkers, however, are deeply insecure. They deal with their insecurities by talking, talking, talking. Talking feels like love to them. They feel loved when they talk and others listen. These people must be handled more carefully. The only way to really solve the problem is to help them with their core needs. We must help them talk less and make them feel good in the process. This can be a real challenge, but no one said teaching a small group would be easy. Compliment them. Praise them. Make heroes out of them. Tell them you want everyone else to share as freely as they do, but that, in order to accomplish this, you need them to be quiet. Take them to lunch. Don't reject them. Don't crush them. Love them.

> The needs of the many outweigh the needs of the few.

The needs of the many outweigh the needs of the few. An overly talkative person can single-handedly ruin an entire class. So do the brave thing. Do the loving thing. Do whatever it takes to create an atmosphere in which everyone can talk and learn. Love the person who talks too much, but love the group as well. Do what it takes to keep everyone talking, but do it with grace. If you do not love that person as Christ does, you will never help him or her to change. People only change in an atmosphere of love, so show overtalkers grace and truth. Grace is about telling them they are accepted. Truth is about telling them they are hurting the class and need to control their tongues.

Prayer in the Classroom

Contrary to what we often think, too much prayer in a classroom can kill the disciple-making process as quickly as someone who talks too much. Prayer is one of those things that we naturally think we should be doing more of. We can hardly imagine that it's possible to pray enough, much less entertain the idea that we could pray too much. We may secretly imagine that God wants us to be on our knees all the time. But that cannot be what 1 Thessalonians 5:17—"Pray without ceasing" (NRSV)— really means.

We cannot be on our knees all the time and still do all that God has given us to do. In the same way, we cannot spend all our time together praying and still reach the goal that God has set before us, namely, life-changing learning.

Admittedly, praying too much is not the worst of our problems. For most of us, it isn't a problem at all, and the very suggestion will probably send several copies of this book across the room in disgust. Before you toss me aside, please read on.

Question: Have you ever been in a class that made announcements, took prayer requests, chatted about and prayed for each one, looked at the clock, and then listened to the teacher say, "Well we don't have much time left. Let me just summarize what we were going to cover"? In my experience, this happens all too often. This kind of teaching doesn't make disciples. In order to transform sinners into saints, we must confront people with the truth. We must show them the gap between where they are and where they should be. Summarizing a few things we were going to say after the hour is spent simply will not work. Teaching is more than telling, remember?

Too much prayer in a classroom can kill the disciple-making process.

Even if you prepare and present a solid lesson, there is a chance that the group still won't get it. That is a given. We try to prepare so that it doesn't happen very often. But if you do nothing more than summarize what you were going to teach, the chances that anyone will learn anything are almost nil. You will have sacrificed the disciple-making process on the altar of prayer. Setting aside a lesson occasionally because the prayer time is especially authentic and powerful is wonderful. But it is also wonderful to expose people to the life-changing Word of God nearly every week.

Now let's look at the fine print. In my experience, prayer is rarely the problem. Prayer requests are. Some sharing of prayer requests is good. It builds community, deepens relationships. But when talking endlessly about someone's ingrown toenail displaces the teaching of the Word of God, we have a problem.

Now the good news. This is an easy problem to solve. It amazes me how few find the answer. Some teachers try to limit the time for prayer requests and prayer, but this rarely works. No one actually stops in the middle of prayer and says, "Time's up!" In addition, trying to hurry people along doesn't work. It just irritates people. So what is the answer? The answer is simple: Take prayer requests last. Decide how much time you want to spend on prayer, appoint a timekeeper, ask that person to warn you five minutes before it's time to pray and again when the teaching time is up, then pray last. You will find that talking about someone's toenail is not nearly as interesting at the end of the hour as it was at the beginning. There will be fewer comments and much less (dare I say it?) gossip.

Don't think of this as manipulative or as placing a low value on prayer. It isn't. It is a simple principle of time management: Do what you need to do before you do what you would like to do. The truth is, much of what goes on in the name of prayer requests is the simple, innocent sharing of lives. There's nothing wrong with that, but we need teaching as well.

One teacher, Mike Stone, told me that his class passes around a prayer-request sheet during class. After the sheet makes it around the room, the class secretary steps out and makes copies. Then, during the last ten minutes of class, people pray over these requests. Mike also files these prayer requests in a folder and asks people about them later on—either before or after class, not during class time. Then he frequently reports how God has answered these prayer requests during class.

Certain things in life can't be rushed. They need a leisurely pace to allow a process to run its course. Cut short the process, and the results are nearly always less than satisfactory. Take making bread, for example. Or worship. Or intimate time with your spouse. Certain processes don't come out the same when they are hurried. Teaching is another example. You simply cannot rush it. You cannot accomplish in a dozen ten-minute time slots what you can do in one forty-five-minute block of time.

Of course, if the group really is engaged in prayer—heads bowed and on their faces before God, talking to their Father—I have no problem with that. But let's call a spade a spade. Let's not call it prayer when it is really prayer requests or, in some cases, small talk and gossip.

Some have suggested that we not take prayer requests at all, that we take our prayer requests directly to God. You may want to do that. For example, you might give everyone thirty seconds to think of one prayer request and then ask each person to silently pray for the request of the person on his or her right. That way every request is shared with and taken to the one person who can make a difference—God. Whatever you do, jealously guard your time in learning and applying God's Word together.

It frustrates the group and the leader when a significant amount of time is not given to God's Word. People come to learn. Offering prayer-shortened lessons is like running a restaurant that has great service, great atmosphere, a great location, and great prices but very small portions. People walk away unsatisfied.

There will be a few people who will miss the extended prayer times. (They are generally the ones who kept the conversation going in the first place.) In most cases, these people want time to

Certain things in life can't be rushed.

share their thoughts and comments because they simply like to verbalize. So if you move the prayer-request time to the end, you may hear them publicly complain. Thinking that the solution to the world's problems is more talk, they may fight you about putting the prayer requests at the end. They may even cloak this in some kind of God-talk. Be firm. This is what leadership is about. The needs of the many outweigh the needs of the few or of the one. Those, however, who come to learn will rarely complain about the group investing too little time in Bible study. They will just silently walk and stay away. They didn't come for an hour of gabbing, and they won't come back when that is all they find.

It is that serious. People really will stay away, and why shouldn't they if all we do is engage in religious chitchat? Disciple-making depends on providing enough time nearly every week for people to learn and apply God's Word. So don't fritter away your time with small talk. Remember, "When words are many, sin is not absent, but he who holds his tongue is wise" (Proverbs 10:19). Maximize your time. Take prayer requests last.

Reading Your Students

One of the things teachers discover early on is that they stand in front of a different class every time they teach. This is part of what makes teaching both exciting and frightening. So to maintain a good learning environment, you must learn to "read" the people in your group every time you teach.

Classes vary from week to week for several fundamental reasons. First, different people show up each week. The exact combination is seldom the same, and it is difficult, if not impossible, to create and sustain the same spirit when the personal chemistry is constantly changing. One person can often make a big difference in the mix. For example, I have prepared lessons to meet the needs of certain people whom I thought would be present. When they were not, it changed the flavor of the soup.

Second, even if the same group of people were to show up week after week on a fairly consistent basis, they are never really the same from one week to the next. All of us bring a certain amount of mental and emotional baggage to class (that includes teachers as well), and even faithful, long-time class members are seldom in exactly the same frame of mind all of the time.

Why is all of this important? Teaching is about connecting the truth with the learner. To do this, you must know both the truth and the learner. Disciple-making teachers know where their students are and where they live (not the addresses of their homes, but where they are on their spiritual journeys). You need to be a student of your students, studying and mentally noting where they are, both in class and in their lives.

The first way to know your students is to spend time with them. Good teachers invest their lives in the lives of their students. They invite them to their homes and go out to eat with them. If you want to know what difference a lesson is going to make in someone's life on Monday morning, you need to know where that person will be and what he or she will be doing on Monday morning (and beyond).

The more you know about your students (would-be disciples), the more sensitive you should be to the central issues in their lives. We are dealing with real people who face real issues in their lives. For example...

• Has anyone gone through an especially traumatic divorce after a twenty-year marriage?

• Is one of the couples in the group suffering from a job loss or financial distress?

• Is one of the members of the group struggling with an eating disorder?

• Is a couple grappling with the emotional roller coaster linked with infertility?

As a teacher, you should never seek to discover intimate details out of a perverse sense of curiosity. But even if you don't, you may find out more about people's lives than you really want to know. When these sorts of details do come to light, we need to be good stewards of that information.

Being a good steward involves at least two things. First, it means that you must never publicly disclose information shared with you in confidence. If a group member voluntarily shares a personal struggle or situation, that is fine. But never, never, never suddenly call on someone and ask, "Mary how did you and Al feel when you lost your baby?"

> You need to be a student of your students.

However, details about people that are common knowledge and are not of a confidential or embarrassing nature are always fair game in class. In fact, using this kind of information properly can draw class members, especially the more reserved ones, into discussions and helps keep the group's attention focused.

For example, if you were teaching a lesson on a Christian's obligation to be salt and light in the world, you might draw a usually quiet member into the lesson by asking, "Ann, I know that you work for XYZ Incorporated. How would your supervisors and co-workers respond if they saw you reading your Bible at your desk during the lunch hour? Would you feel comfortable doing so?" By asking a question or series of questions such as this, you can personalize the lesson and attempt to bridge the gap between what people learn in class and what they face in the real world outside of class.

A second aspect of knowing your students is learning how to read their body language in class. You can develop the basis for this ability by spending enough time with them to know what is a normal expression, a typical reaction, and the like. Paying close attention to people's body language will often tell you how well they understand and whether they agree.

As a teacher, I always like to have two or three easily visible "reactors"—people who respond demonstratively when you hit one of their hot buttons. Their reactions may be facial—raised eyebrows or questioning looks—or they may suddenly sit up straight and scoot to the front of their chairs, their mouths open slightly in anticipation of saying something. However they respond, reactors provide a teacher with immediate feedback or even serve as catalysts for classroom discussions.

Reactors are easy to read. You generally know exactly what they are thinking and feeling because they tell you in so many words. Do not, however, let reactors dominate discussions to the detriment of the rest of the class. If it is the custom in your class for people to raise their hands to speak (many children's classes do this, but some adult classes do it as well), reactors will be easy to spot because their hands will always be up. Some teachers deal with these people simply by trying to ignore them when they raise their hands. Sometimes this works, but many reactors blurt out their thoughts anyway.

To avoid this, you can either have people discuss questions in groups of four or five (reminding them that every group member gets a chance to talk) or act as if questions addressed to the entire group are a scarce commodity that must be rationed. Then you say, "David, I only have a few questions today. Do you want to answer yours now or wait till later?" My experience has been that while these people might not understand what you are doing, most of them do not have terribly fragile egos and are not offended by your honesty.

Reactors can also have their opinions exploited, in a positive sense, to serve the purposes of discussion. Allow the reactors to respond and express their views; then turn to the group or to one member of the group and ask, "How do you feel about what Helen just said?" After a little coaxing and practice, people will become comfortable responding to the positions taken by these reactors.

In the end, the biggest challenge for you as a teacher is reading people who neither show visible reactions nor speak up. These group members sometimes have the most profound insights, but because they are introverted or new to the class they do not volunteer many answers. The goal for every disciple-making teacher should be "no spectators." People learn the most when they are involved in the process.

To involve people, you may want to make frequent use of small-group discussions with report-back times. Or you may call on people directly who do not share voluntarily, but this requires sensitivity. The easiest way to do this is to ask a simple "What does the text say?" question. For example, I might ask, "Bill, according to Romans 12:1, what is a reasonable response on our part to God's mercy to us?" If someone else is a deep thinker but not a big talker, I might ask a more profound question: "Jane, what do you think it means, practically, to be a living sacrifice?"

If you know group members well enough—if you are a student of your students—you will be able to monitor and manage the learning environment to develop a pattern of maximum participation. This involves getting the thinkers and the reactors, the introverts and the extroverts, the new Christians and the "old timers" all committed to the process of learning from and teaching each other, all under the leadership of the Holy Spirit and you, a disciple-making teacher.

When Not to Teach

Sometimes the most spiritual and helpful thing you can do for a group is to set aside the lesson. Sometimes, if you know people in the group well and are reading the situation in class, you will set aside the lesson to deal with an issue that surfaced earlier in the week or even during class. Sometimes you need to pray. There are times when you may want to spend the hour planning and cultivating relationships within the group. Disciple-making teachers know when not to teach.

Disciple-making teachers do not teach because they have a need to talk, though in a very real sense they do have an internal

People learn the most when they are involved in the process.

need to proclaim truth. They feel some affinity with Paul, who wrote: "Yet when I preach the gospel, I cannot boast, for I am compelled to preach. Woe to me if I do not preach the gospel!" (1 Corinthians 9:16). Disciple-making teachers are so excited about the truth that they cannot keep from telling it. But they don't let their need to speak get in the way of the disciple-making process. The goal is to make disciples, not to teach lessons. Occasionally, other concerns must take priority over teaching.

At times people will mention needs, either before or during class, that call for the lesson to be set aside. You may want to teach an entirely different lesson based on the needs of the group. The needs you anticipated when you planned your lesson may not be the actual needs of the group.

One of the great things about small-group work is that it's flexible. We can teach to felt needs that are on the table at the time. We can reach people when they are at a teachable moment. Far better to teach the group on issues that relate to their current lives than to teach a lesson that, theoretically, they will need to know someday. For one thing, if you teach this way, you can be sure you will always have people's undivided attention. It is easy to get and keep a group's attention when you talk about how the Bible relates to them now.

Sometimes the most spiritual and helpful thing you can do for a group is to set aside the lesson.

For example, suppose someone comes to you before class and says, "Please ask God to give us wisdom. Our four-year-old is out of control. We have tried everything, but we just can't seem to get a grip on him." At times you will jot that down, pray for it, and teach what you prepared. If, however, you know that others in the group have struggled or are struggling with the same issue, you might want to set aside your lesson and deal with it then and there.

You might even ask the person who asked for prayer to share his or her problem with the rest of the class. Then say, "Let's talk about that. What does the Bible teach us about how to discipline our children?" Let people talk. Share what you know. Ask group members to share their insights, whether from experience or books that they've read. Whatever you do, don't let this teachable moment pass. Not only will this be more interesting to the person who made the request, the rest of the group will find it more interesting as well. Talking about what the Bible says about real-life problems is far more compelling than discussing the Bible and some hypothetical situation. Offer people information, inspiration, and strategies that can change their Monday mornings this Monday morning. Seize the moment!

If you follow up on the discussion the next time you meet, you will cause the level of life-change to go up even more. You can do this by asking people if they had any reflections on what the group discussed and how they were able to implement the ideas and the applications that were offered the previous lesson.

If the topic really hits a hot button, I would even consider setting aside several weeks or even months to deal with the felt need of the group. Of course, it must be the felt need of the entire group, but if everyone were struggling with parenting, I would set aside whatever we were studying so the entire group could work its way through a book such as James Dobson's, *The Strong-Willed Child* or one of Gary Smalley's video series. Remember: You are there to teach people, not a lesson.

Doing this shows people that you care about them. If you are interested enough in their lives to set aside a lesson you worked hard preparing, they will get a lot more interested in what you have to say. But they must know that you care about them more than you care about presenting your material. The lesson has no need to be taught, but the group has desperate needs. The lesson has no needs at all. The lesson must serve the group, not the other way around.

Sometimes important issues will arise in the middle of class. For example, what would you do if someone unexpectedly said, "I've been wondering lately. How can we be sure that the Bible is reliable?" You could say, "That's a good question, and I'm sure that we will get to it someday. In the meantime, we are here today to talk about John 4. Will you open your Bibles..." You could say that, but I wouldn't recommend it. It is far better to try to answer the question on the spot, to get with this person privately later on, or to agree to present a better answer next week. Whatever you do, listen to people if you want them to listen to you.

Obviously, it must be an important issue to justify setting aside a lesson. It doesn't happen every week in the classes I teach. We often take short, five or ten minute detours to deal with issues that arise, but rarely do we set aside the entire lesson to discuss something else. Occasionally, though, we need to.

One advantage of teaching over a long period of time is that you become better at fielding unexpected questions. A new teacher may struggle to address anything other than what he or she prepared to teach that day. An experienced teacher, however, can dig deeply into a reservoir of helpful information from books previously read and lessons previously taught. This enables an

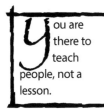
You are there to teach people, not a lesson.

experienced teacher to deal with a question such as the reliability of the Bible on the spur of the moment.

There are even occasions when I think it is best not to teach (or even plan to teach) at all. Occasionally the needs of the group will be so great that you should set aside the lesson to pray. Sometimes it is profitable to spend time evaluating the group and how well it is making disciples. We need to ask from time to time how people are doing in their relationships with God and what they think of the group. We need to look at graphs on the growth of the group and evaluate how well we are obeying the Great Commission. This is especially useful at the end of a year because it encourages the group to set some goals for the following year.

Sometimes we should take time in class to discuss and plan ways to enrich relationships within the group. Remember—your group is not just a class; it is a basic Christian community. It is the Body of Christ learning and sharing life together, so it is OK to occasionally take some time to work on these matters. At times you'll want to do this at another time, and those who are interested can come. But if you need to take the time in class, I would encourage you to do so.

These should be the exceptions. Day in and day out, how-ever, we should be challenging people with God's Word. It is the truth, not announcements, that sets us free (John 8:32). We are transformed by the renewing of our minds (Romans 12:2), not by planning fun group fellowships. People come to be fed. We should not disappoint them. Although there will be exceptions, day in and day out we should be serving up choice morsels of a spiritually rich diet.

So how can you know how to set this balance? How can you know how often you should not teach a lesson or not teach at all? I would ask the group from time to time how they feel about this. Give them some choices. Find out what the Holy Spirit is saying to them. Do they feel they are spending enough time in the Word together, or do they think they are dabbling in other things too much?

If you want a rough estimate, I probably set aside the lesson to teach something else once or twice a year, and every year or two we may not have a lesson at all. That's been my experience. What is more important is that you and your class follow God.

Laughter

Providing a setting in which people laugh freely is an important part of creating a positive learning environment. Moreover, disciple-making teachers learn, either through trial and error or through teacher training classes, that humor is one of the most common and effective devices to get people's attention and to drive home key points during the class.

Laughter is a sign of a positive group life. Groups that enjoy being together laugh together. It is much more difficult to get a new group laughing than it is to get a group that knows one another well to laugh together. In healthy groups, it is sometimes hard to stop the laughter. Where people know they are among friends, laughter is common.

Laughter is not only important to group life, it is also a preview of life in heaven (see Luke 6:21). When we laugh here, we enjoy a taste of heaven above. However, teachers must understand some things about themselves and their students in order to use humor effectively.

> People come to be fed. We should not disappoint them.

First, the most effective disciple-making teachers are students of themselves. They understand differences in teaching styles, and they have an accurate assessment of their most comfortable and effective styles. They can tell you in twenty-five words or less, "In most cases I like to present the lesson by…" This does not mean that effective teachers are so committed to one style of presentation that they never deviate from it. In fact, they are effective because they are flexible and adaptable enough to respond to changing conditions and emotions in the class.

Knowing one's teaching style is particularly crucial with regard to the use of humor in class. There are at least four groups of teachers when it comes to using humor in class:

- One group uses humor very naturally throughout the lesson. With these kinds of teachers, jokes, funny stories, wordplays, and puns occur somewhat spontaneously and appear almost second nature to them.
- A second group of teachers often includes humorous material at key points during the lesson. They think to themselves, "When we get here, I'm going to tell the story or joke about…" These teachers may not think of themselves as being naturally funny, but they work at it because it serves a purpose in their teaching.

- A third group of teachers are not humorous themselves, but they enjoy it when group members liven and lighten the lesson with a bit of healthy humor.
- The fourth group of teachers try to be humorous, but with little success. Their attempts at humor often provoke sighs, rolling of people's eyes, or even gasps from the class. They would be better off to follow the example of the third group.

> **W**hen we laugh here, we enjoy a taste of heaven above.

The challenge for the teacher is to know what his or her teaching style is, both generally and specifically as it relates to the use of humor. Knowing and understanding which style seems to match one's tendencies can help the disciple-making teacher maximize his or her strengths while avoiding any dangers.

When (and When Not) to Use Humor

There are a few strategic times during class when a teacher can use humor effectively. The practice of many preachers, and one often copied by teachers as well, is to tell a joke at the beginning of the message. This is designed as an icebreaker, a means of relaxing the listeners (and usually the preacher/teacher as well) and of focusing people's attention. Humor used in this way can be topical (related to the lesson) or not, since the primary purpose is not necessarily to make a point.

But teachers can also use humor to good effect during the lesson. Humor at this point typically serves two functions: to emphasize a particular point or to ease tensions, if it is helpful to do so. (As a teacher, you should remember that there are times when a good dose of tension is healthy. It keeps people listening and the discussion focused.)

Perhaps an illustration of humor during class would be helpful at this point. In a lesson on the book of Job, the class was asked to name Job's three "friends." (They had been discussed the week before, so this was a review.) The students named Eliphaz, Bildad, and Zophar. After the last name the teacher responded, "zo-far, zo-good!" Of course, the class let out a loud groan, but two things are important to remember. First, when you use puns or wordplays, the louder the groan, the more your point struck home. In other words, the students got it. Second, because the humor was topical, the class related it to the point at hand. The teacher had given them a mental "hook" on which to hang this information.

Sometimes humor can drive home an especially important point in a particularly "pointed" way. We have all had the experience of rolling on the floor in laughter, then discovering a dagger in our side when we finally stopped laughing. The speaker put it there while the anesthesia of laughter was at its peak. At times, laughter is an effective tool for making a point.

Humor can also be used to relieve tension. As I explained earlier, some tension is good because tension causes change. But sometimes, when the mood is too heavy, a spontaneous outburst of laughter can break the tension and allow the Holy Spirit to do his work.

The third time to use humor, although it is less common than the first two, is at the end of the lesson. The class is generally pretty serious by this point, so the teacher must be careful in using humor here. You do not want people walking away from the class feeling that the lesson really wasn't important because you ended with a joke. Use humor at the end of the lesson, but only if it drives home, rather than damages, your main point.

Just as there are times to use humor in teaching, there are also times not to use it. For example, if you are known as a person with a keen sense of humor and being funny comes naturally (you not only know the latest jokes, but you can also tell jokes on just about any subject at the drop of a hat), you should beware of coming across as frivolous or insincere. Be es-pecially careful not to tell inappropriate jokes (test them out on "sensitive" listeners first) or to tell jokes at inappropriate times.

By the same token, if you struggle with trying to be funny, your attempts at humor may detract from your natural teaching style and the learning objectives you have envisioned for the class. A good way to check your HQ (humor quotient) is to ask your spouse and children. They can be brutally honest at times. Another measure of your HQ is the extent to which you can remember punch lines. The rule of thumb is: if you can't (remember), don't (tell jokes). If you have a low HQ, my advice is fairly simple: Do not try to be something you are not.

How to Use Humor

The safest way to inject humor into a lesson is through topical humor—jokes that relate to the subject at hand. However, these jokes should never refer to any group member, either by name or by implication. As a teacher, you also need to know which topics are (or should be) taboo within the group. For instance, jokes about divorce or husband-wife relationships may be particularly stinging to some group members. Avoid harmful jokes at all times.

Personal humor (that which singles out a group member) should always be used with great caution, but don't avoid it completely. Rather, know the people in class well enough to use personal humor well.

A recent experience of mine illustrates what I mean. Some time ago, I asked class members a question about something or someone in the lesson. The man who answered is a very perceptive, outgoing, and typically vocal member of the class. But the answer he gave to this question was uncharacteristically off-the-wall. In this case, I had known him long enough to anticipate his reaction, so I looked at his wife and said, "Don't let John answer any more questions today." The class reaction was spontaneous and unrestrained laughter, and John was among those laughing hardest. My point is: I knew John well enough to know that I could get away with this remark.

If I had directed the same comment at others in the class, people would have thought that I was being cynical or mean. But with John I could follow up my comment by asking, "Would you like to take another shot at answering that question?" and he felt perfectly comfortable doing so.

> If you have a low HQ, my advice is fairly simple: Do not try to be something you are not.

One of the best ways to use personal humor in a nonthreatening way is to tell the class something funny (or even embarrassing) that happened to you. This keeps others from feeling uncomfortable about being the object of everyone's laughter, and it helps show that you as a teacher are just like everyone else.

Humor can contribute to a positive learning environment, so use it as best you can. Remember that disciple-making teachers use humor most effectively when they know themselves and their students well.

Notes

[1] The questions I use in teaching are available on the World Wide Web at www.joshhunt.com. There are a number of similar resources on the market, such as The Serendipity Bible (NIV) and New Testament LessonMaker (NavPress).

[2] Robert B. Cialdini, Ph.D., Influence: How and Why People Agree to Things (New York: Quill, 1984), 115–116.

[3] Taken from a speech delivered by Martin Luther King, Jr., on August 28, 1963.

[4] To learn more about active learning, see Thom and Joani Schultz, Why Nobody Learns Much of Anything at Church: And How to Fix It (Loveland, CO: Group Publishing, 1993), 105-139.

Section Four:
The Teacher Outside of Class

	Outside of Class	In Class
Teacher	Preparation	Presentation
Learner	Lifestyles	Learning

Whole-Brained Preparation

In order to present the right kind of lesson in class (so people learn in class and live as disciples outside of class), the teacher needs to engage in the right kind of preparation. In order to know what questions people need to discuss, what learning experiences will help people learn, and what central point needs to be repeated time and time again, the teacher needs to prepare each and every lesson carefully and thoughtfully.

> Preparation at its best uses both halves of the brain.

As I see it, there are two ways to prepare a lesson. Quite frankly, the way I learned to prepare is not the best way. A teacher can crank out a lesson as a matter of discipline (as I was taught), or a lesson can bubble forth from a life that is happily meditating on the truth of God. Preparation at its best does a little of each. Preparation at its best uses both halves of the brain.

Left-Brained Preparation

Left-brained preparation is a good start. Left-brained preparation involves studying, digging, analyzing, working, writing, rewriting, thinking, and rewriting. Like it or not, you simply need to do this. You read commentaries, consult Bible dictionaries, look up key words in a concordance, and consider how those words are used elsewhere. Your brain processes, compares, contrasts, and synthesizes all this information. There's nothing wrong with this. God created the left side of your brain. Let me be clear: God loves your left brain.

But the best lessons I have prepared did not rely on this method alone. Certainly, I engaged in study, research, and analysis—all left-brained processes. But preparation at its best makes full use of both halves of the brain.

Whole-Brained Preparation

Whole-brained preparation is fairly loosey-goosey. It is hard to state a formula for whole-brained preparation, just as it would be difficult to come up with a color-by-numbers approach to painting the Mona Lisa. Still, there is some logic to the creative process. The process works something like this.

Study for a while using traditional left-brained methods. Read the biblical text several times. Bombard it with questions. Consult the commentaries to find out what others have said about the text.

But don't get too serious about it. Don't feel as though you need to form your conclusions at this point. Just get your motor going and let it idle.

Then set aside the lesson and do something completely unrelated. Treat yourself to some casual reading—perhaps something by Chuck Swindoll or Max Lucado. If you prefer, read Louis L'Amour or Tom Peters.

After a while, try to outline what you want to present in class. Again, don't feel too pressured. If you can't think of a good outline, don't worry. If you teach on Sunday, you should be doing this no later than Tuesday, so you still have plenty of time for the lesson to come together.

Return to your left-brained approach. Read the text. Study it. Dig into it. Spend some time trying to identify the "big idea" of the text and the biggest need in your group that relates to this central idea. Ask lots of questions of the text. Use your study helps to discover answers, but focus on application, not biblical trivia.

Then set it aside again. Play with your kids. Go work in the yard for a while. Chat with your spouse. Read Charles Colson. He may seem terribly convicting, but he has such great stories. That is what you need right now—some good stories.

Work this process back and forth. You may want to spend thirty minutes or so in formal study or reading each day, but you need to be constantly pondering the biblical text and figuring out how it relates to the people in your group. As you drive, walk, exercise, and so on, let the ideas in the text percolate in your brain.

Discuss the text with several people during the week. Try some of your questions out on them. Live the text. Make it a part of your life this week.

Make another trial run at the lesson, maybe writing out questions for people to discuss or jotting down ideas for learning experiences.

Do some more left-brained preparation.

Read something by James Dobson or C.S. Lewis.

Work around the house or in the yard.

Try again to come up with a lesson plan.

When I use this approach (I would rarely use more than a third of the steps above), the lesson will often come to me fully formed, ready to teach in about ten minutes. At that point I can walk into class and teach it. Anything else I do is a bonus. I generally continue to use the same process to refine the lesson, and occasionally this will involve more than a minor revision. Usually, however, I just stir the ingredients until the whole stew comes together at once.

Sometimes the lesson will come to me in the middle of the night, just before I go to bed, or when I first wake up. I have also written out a number of solid lessons on napkins at restaurants. When this happens, it is one of the grand experiences of the Christian life. I feel as though the Holy Spirit is just flowing through me. Ideas come so quickly that I can barely write them down.

Whole-brained preparation is much easier and more effective than simply grinding out a lesson plan. In fact, it seems like no work at all. I have found few things to be more fun. More important, however, whole-brained preparation produces far better results than simply using half of one's brain because it synthesizes four things:

- the lesson text or topic,
- the needs of the group,
- a life of personal growth, and
- this week's creative reading.

When you put these ingredients into the stew, the lesson nearly always comes out richer than if you had relied on some "out-of-the-can" variety.

> **W**hole-brained preparation is much easier and more effective than simply grinding out a lesson plan.

There is, of course, an element of risk. What if it gets late in the week and that magical moment has not yet come? What if you don't have anything to say, and it's the day before class? That is when you simply have to grind it out. You can probably do fine at that, but it's far better to let the right side of your brain get in on the fun.

I believe this is why the Bible encourages us to meditate on God's Word. For example, Psalm 1:1-3 states...

> Blessed is the man who does not walk in the counsel of the wicked or stand in the way of sinners or sit in the seat of mockers. But his delight is in the law of the Lord, and on his law he *meditates* day and night. He is like a tree planted by streams of water, which yields its fruit in season and whose leaf does not wither. Whatever he does prospers.

In my opinion, meditation is the domain of the right side of the brain. So disciple-making teachers adhere to the biblical principle of meditation when they engage in right-brained preparation.

The goal of whole-brained preparation is to take all the details of a biblical text and to distill them into one central idea that people can learn and apply to their lives. All the preparation points to this one idea, and all our teaching methods—whether questions, learning experiences, videos, or something else—should support this central idea. Because this is so important, the next section will discuss how to identify and develop a central teaching idea.

We Teach So Little Because We Try to Teach So Much

Sam Shaw is one of the finest preachers I have ever heard, the best I personally know. Sam is a gifted communicator who has honed his natural skills into a fine art through constant work. A wall in his office is covered with books on preaching, teaching, and communication. A careful look at these books reveals that he has read and marked in them all. He constantly listens to tapes by the best preachers in the country. Not content to rely on his natural talent alone, which is substantial, he constantly pushes himself to do better. Every week, when he steps up to the plate, he swings for the fence, and he regularly puts the ball over. In five years I never saw him pop up. I kept waiting. Each week I wondered if this sermon might be a dud. It never was. He always presented extremely good sermons, often incredible ones.

One day, while I was working on a sermon of my own, I asked Sam for some help. "I have a good idea here, but I just need a little more material to flesh it out. Any ideas?" "Tons of them. I could give you hours worth of ideas if you wanted them. You see, the easiest thing in the world is to preach an hour-long sermon. There's plenty of good material to do that. The real challenge is to preach a twenty-minute sermon. The key to communication is knowing what not to say. It is knowing what to leave out."

Sam excels as a preacher because he knows what to leave in and what to leave out. Sam is a master at the one-point sermon. For Sam, every sermon is a one-point sermon. If a sermon contains three points, they are there simply to support the one central idea.

> "The key to communication is knowing what not to say. It is knowing what to leave out."
> —Sam Shaw

He used to test himself by asking his kids, who were in grade school at the time, what the main idea of a message was. He figured that if Charlie, his third-grader could get it, he had done pretty well. Sam knows the value of focus and concentration. He used to speak of it as "the big idea."

People often learn so little because we try to teach too much. We could all learn a lesson from Sam: Less is more. To teach well, concentrate the lesson around one big idea. Make everything in the lesson a servant to that big idea.

To support and convey the big idea, Sam asks and answers two questions about nearly every topic: "Why?" and "How?" In many cases, the first half of his message will deal with "Why?" and the second half will answer "How?" People need to know why in order to care about the how. They must also know how or the why won't do them much good. Why and how. Why and how. Every week, help the people in your class understand why and how. Here are few examples to show you what I mean:

Why we should have a servant's heart.
How we can develop a servant's heart.

Why we should prepare for Christ's return.
How we can be ready for Christ's return.

Why and how. Why should we tell people why and how? Because it makes for interesting communication. Because people want to know why and how. Because it helps people become disciples.

All your preparation should drive every lesson toward one central idea, toward one big idea around which all of the lesson will revolve. As you read, study, meditate, pray, and think, you should search for the one main idea that will be the focus of the entire lesson. Once this main idea is in place, everything you plan will flow out of it. The big idea is the intersection between a biblical text and people's needs. Teaching at its best connects people's needs with the Bible.

Normally, the big idea of a lesson will correspond to the central idea of the text. If, for example, you were studying 1 Corinthians 13, you would probably want to help people discover the importance and the qualities of love. If you were studying Hebrews 11, you might want people to learn what faith is and why they need it. Because the big idea of a lesson and the central idea of its text are usually the same, your preparation should involve carefully studying the text to discover exactly what it teaches. Ask yourself two questions: "What is the main theme or topic of this passage?" *and* "What does this text say about that topic?" Boil down your thoughts into a single sentence; then translate that sentence into a lesson idea that will be relevant and meaningful to the people in your class.

> The big idea is the intersection between a biblical text and people's needs.

Occasionally a big idea may arise from a secondary point in the text. For example, I once taught a lesson from Galatians 2, which records Paul's rebuke of Peter for denying the essence of grace by refusing to eat with non-Jews. In this case, I chose to teach a lesson on the right way to correct a fellow Christian. This may or may not be the main point of the text, but it fit the needs of the class better than the other options. Normally, however, it is wisest and safest to make the big idea of a lesson the same as the central point of the text.

Once the big idea is in place, everything else flows out of it. From here, the task is pretty straightforward. You write out discussion questions that lead people to the big idea. You explore the possibility of using things people can touch and feel to experience the big idea. You look for illustrations that support the main idea. You think of specific applications that flow from the big idea. You try to think up a catchy repeated phrase that will capture and convey the essence of the big idea. You check to see if there are any videos you could use to support the big idea.

In disciple-making teaching, everything revolves around the big idea. Your initial preparation seeks to discover the big idea. Then, when the big idea is in place, you use every resource and teaching method at your disposal to support the big idea. This is the way my friend Sam Shaw did it, and it is a great way for you to prepare effective lessons as well.

Reading Books

I wonder how you came to read this book. Did you find it on the shelf of a bookstore? Did you notice it in a catalog or read about it in a book review? Or did your pastor or Christian education director hand it to you as assigned reading? If someone did hand it to you, how did you feel when the cover hit your hand? Did you say to yourself:

- "I'm open to that—maybe I'll learn something";
- "Oh, no—another boring book on teaching";
- "This is just one more thing I have to do!" or
- "Ugh!"

If your response was anything less than the first one, you may be in trouble. Disciple-making teachers are readers. They are learners. Remember: The biblical word translated "disciple" means "learner." Disciple-making teachers are consumers, processors, and dispensers of truth. A teacher who does not read is like an ice company that doesn't take in water. If you are not learning today, you will find it difficult to teach tomorrow. People grow bored of hearing the same tired stories. There must be an abundance of truth coming in.

Nearly every week you should be able to say, "I was reading a new book the other day and the author pointed out…" Paul recognized the importance of reading. For example, he instructed Timothy, "When you come, bring the cloak that I left with Carpus at

Troas, and my scrolls, especially the parchments"
(2 Timothy 4:13). Do you hear what Paul is saying?
Winter is coming. It's cold, and Paul needs his heavy
coat. But he also left some books—parchments and
scrolls—that he asks Timothy to bring along as well.
Paul seems just as concerned to have access to his
books as he does to retrieve his heavy cloak that will
keep him warm. Paul valued books. That reflects the
heart of a teacher. Teachers are readers.

> a teacher who does not read is like an ice com-pany that doesn't take in water.

My friend Bill Sloan inspired me to write my first
book. He also inspired me to read my first book. By the time I was a
sophomore in college, I had not read a single book outside of
assigned class work. I casually mentioned this to Bill one day, who
responded, "Josh, that's terrible. Just think of all the knowledge you
are missing out on." God spoke to me through those words. Since I
knew nothing about books, I asked Bill to suggest a title. Bill
pointed me to Rosalind Rinker's *Prayer: Conversing With God*. I read
it, I loved it, and I can say in all candor that my life was permanently
altered by reading that single book. Immediately I read William
Barclay's commentary on Philippians, then several biographies of
Christians such as D. L. Moody, Charles Wesley, and George Mueller.
By this time I was hooked. There has probably not been a day since
that I have not been in the middle of one or more books. I normally
keep four or five going at the same time, but I only finish about half
the books I start. Life is too short to read two hundred pages of a
book that should have been only one hundred pages long.

Reading has another advantage. It presents a positive example
to the people in the group. One of your goals for your group should
be to make readers out of them. Even if you did not teach them
anything in class all year but you inspired them to read a half dozen
good books during that same time, you will have served them well.

As I was considering how disciples are made, I asked myself
what has caused me to grow in the faith. A major influence in my life
has been the books I have read. The sermons I have heard, the
classes I have attended, the quiet times I have enjoyed all have
contributed to my growth. Still, books may have been the single
most influential factor in the transforming of my mind.

Books put us in touch with the greatest thoughts of the
greatest hearts and minds of the greatest people God has used. If
you could sit down with Billy Graham for six hours and have him tell
you what it means to live for God, would you take the opportunity?
You can. Read his books. The same is true of Bill Hybels, Chuck
Swindoll, Max Lucado, R. C. Sproul, J. I. Packer, John Calvin, Martin
Luther, and Augustine. As a teacher, you can find specific ideas and
help from people who have thought hard about issues such as

prayer, marriage, sharing one's faith, and living as a disciple of Christ. Do you really want to be cut off from that source of truth? I don't.

Occasionally you will hear teachers say, "I consult no one else's commentaries. I read no human books. I rely solely on the Holy Spirit and the reading of God's Word." Sounds pious and spiritual, doesn't it? But think about it. What the speaker is actually saying is, "I only care about what the Holy Spirit says to me about this text. I don't care what the Holy Spirit might have said to others through the years." In addition to being spiritually prideful, this is incredibly unwise. People far brighter and more spiritual than I have thought a good deal about the Bible. They have put these thoughts into writing and made them accessible to me. It doesn't seem too smart to cut myself off from this body of truth. To do so in the name of piety would be incredibly dumb.

I often read good books as part of my quiet time. Obviously this does not replace reading the Bible itself, but I have found it a heartwarming experience to read through a few pages of a book such as John Stott's *The Cross of Christ.*

> Christian discipleship is not a state to be attained or a goal to be achieved. It is a process of constant, continual, lifelong learning.

But it gets even better. In this generation we have the opportunity not only to read the thoughts of great Christian thinkers but actually to hear their voices. Consequently, I would advise you to maximize the time you spend in your car by listening to messages from some of God's spokespersons to this generation. Most of the Christian leaders I greatly respect do this, and I have found it rewarding as well. In addition, if you don't enjoy reading all that much, why not learn from one of the many excellent Christian videos that are available today? However you do it, whether through books, tapes, or videos, make sure that you are learning today. If you don't, you may not have anything to teach tomorrow.

In the popular television show *Star Trek: The Next Generation*, the producers portray Captain Jean-Luc Picard reading a book from time to time. It is a flashback of sorts from the highly advanced twenty-fourth century to a rather antiquated technology created during the fifteenth century. The producers are making a statement. They believe that books will still be around four hundred years from now. I think they are right. I don't think CD-ROMs or videos will replace books. I don't think the Internet will replace books. I believe that books will be around for a long time to come. In fact, one might even say that the Bible predicts as much in Ecclesiastes 12:12b: "Of making many books there is no end." I think books will be just as important in the twenty-fourth century as they were when Paul reminded Timothy to bring his cloak and "especially the parchments." Books have always been important to the people of God.

But please understand: This is not all about paper and ink. It is about learning, about growing, about discovery, about changing. It is about living the life of a disciple. Disciples, not to mention disciple-making teachers, are learners. Christian discipleship is not a state to be attained or a goal to be achieved. It is a process of constant, continual, lifelong learning. Discipleship is not about arriving but about becoming a constantly growing person. Books are an important part of that process.

Closing
Thoughts

I Love It!

I love teaching. I love the laughter, the tears, the moments when God breaks in and does something incredible. I love the moments of discovery in class as well as the hours of preparation before class. I love the relationships. I love the outreach. I love the opportunity God has given me. I love the dream.

I love poring over dusty old commentaries. I love discovering a Newsweek article or a Chuck Swindoll story that fits perfectly with this week's lesson. I love it when God orchestrates the circumstances of my life so that I am able to use something that happened this week to teach or illustrate a key point of the lesson. I love getting started early and letting the lesson simmer like rich New Mexico chili. I love pondering, thinking, and praying over a biblical passage.

I enjoy leading the discussion. I love the energy, the animation that fills me whenever I teach. I love asking silly questions that get people talking, laughing, opening up, and getting to know each other. I enjoy opening the Word of God together to see what a text says and what it means to our lives. I love evaluating where we are and where we should be. I love it when the personal stories of those more mature in the faith cast a light on the trail for the rest of us.

Most of all, I love seeing what happens when people really think, really learn. Their eyes brighten. They raise a finger to make a point. They start to speak, then their own inner dialogue pulls them back. They pause to think through the issues further. Then, when the thoughts have fully fermented, they blurt them out without worrying about interrupting what I might be saying: "Well, I think…" Their enthusiasm bubbles over and spills throughout the entire room. They say something that has never been said before. They think thoughts that have never been thought before.

I love seeing people's lives change. I love watching people grow up over time. In a way, it is like watching your kids grow up. Though some part of you may look back fondly to when they were young, to their first steps, their first words, their precarious first attempts to ride a bicycle, we are happy to see them grow. So it is with the heavenly Father. God delights when his children first come to faith. Jesus taught that all of heaven smiles and rejoices when one sinner repents (Luke 15:7). But God delights even more as his children grow to be more like him. God delights when gossips become encouragers, complainers become worshipers, and thieves become givers.

We also delight to watch group members grow up over time. We love to watch them learn to get along with others. We love to see them reading the Bible on their own and discovering truth for themselves. We love it when they discover their gifts and use them to serve others. What a joy to see them become passionate about serving God. We love to see their hearts as well as their checkbooks open for the cause of Christ.

We love to see families that really work. We love to see husbands and wives who really love each other. We love to see couples who know how to nurture their kids. We love to see the church develop into an extended family so that we become uncles and aunts to each other's kids. We love to see singles living their lives as part of a community, part of a family.

This book is an invitation. An invitation for you to love it, too. You probably already do, or you wouldn't have read a book on becoming a disciple-making teacher. Only those who love felling trees take time to sharpen their axes.

But I hope this won't be the last book on teaching that you read. I pray that you will be a lifelong learner, both of God's Word and of the craft of teaching. Teaching is difficult, but with hard work and the enabling of the Holy Spirit, we can do our job well. To that end, I challenge you to engage in a lifelong pursuit of learning how to teach more effectively.

> Only those who love felling trees take time to sharpen their axes.

You see, this book isn't primarily about teaching; it is about love. It is about loving the people in your group enough to skillfully help them learn the truth that will set them free. Nothing else will set them free. Only teachers who love the truth, love their groups, and love the work enough to do it well will help people be set free. I love teaching. I hope that you love it, too.

The Heart of a Teacher

The Bible presents the gift of teaching as a hyphenated gift: pastor-teacher (Ephesians 4:11). Teaching is a part of a larger gift that contains two elements. Consequently, the other side of teaching is pastoring. Pastoring involves being a shepherd who cares for the sheep. It means leading people to the greener pastures when they would rather wander about. "Pastor" is a tender term, a loving term, a term that expresses how God feels about his people. God is also a pastor, a shepherd to his people (Genesis 48:15; Psalm 23:1; John 10:11, 14, 16).

Some teachers try to avoid this. They simply want to present the truth and walk away. But this is not the way of the small-group leader. People want to be loved by their teacher. People need to be loved by their teacher. Truth without love is a medicine that tastes so bad that no one ever wants to take it. Theoretically it could help, but no one ever gets better because they cannot stand to take the medicine. In the same way, people will rarely receive truth unless it is learned within the context of love from a caring shepherd.

Consider Paul's philosophy of ministry, for example. Paul told the church at Thessalonica, "We loved you so much that we were delighted to share with you not only the gospel of God but our lives as well, because you had become so dear to us" (1 Thessalonians 2:8). Disciple-making teachers like Paul give of themselves to their students. They spend time with the people in their class. They have them in their homes. They are at the hospital when their babies are born. They grieve the loss of every job and celebrate every promotion, new job, and new house. They become a pastor to the people in their class.

> Truth without love is a medicine that tastes so bad that no one ever wants to take it.

They treat people just as Paul treated the Thessalonians whom he loved so dearly. Paul explains, "But we were gentle among you, like a mother caring for her little children...We dealt with each of you as a father deals with his own children" (1 Thessalonians 2:7, 11b). Paul cared for the people at Thessalonica as if they were his own children. Disciple-making teachers care for the people in their class in exactly the same way.

This is one reason I become more excited about teaching classes of six people than I do classes of thirty. Granted, there is a certain excitement in teaching a large class, but it is mostly ego. Life-change is inversely proportional to the bigness of the group. The bigger the group, the smaller the change.

For example, I led a small group last night, and only one person showed up. I'll admit, a part of me wanted to cancel. But we didn't, and something happened in that group of two that never happens in a group of thirty. We were completely honest. We developed genuine intimacy. We faced reality. We made direct application of truth to a specific situation. Small groups work best at making disciples when they are small.

Someone with the heart of a disciple-making teacher will love, care for, and get close to the people in his or her group. Become a shepherd to the people in your group. Your teaching will never be the same.

Taking Care of Yourself

In this book, I have sought to challenge you to pursue with passion the high and holy calling of becoming a disciple-making teacher. But before I set down my pen (I don't actually set down my pen; it just sounds more poetic than "turn off my computer."), I want to leave you with one final thought: It is more important to take care of the minister than it is to take care of the ministry. Guard your heart. Guard your schedule. Guard your affections. Guard your marriage. There are a million things that need to be done, but you won't be able to do them all. Do what you can, and be at peace about the rest.

If you have ever flown in an airplane, you have heard the speech about what to do in case the cabin loses pressure: strap on the little yellow cones and plastic bags that drop down from the ceiling. They will provide oxygen for you to breath. Question: If you are traveling with a child, whose mask do you put on first—yours or your child's?

> It is more important to take care of the minister than it is to take care of the ministry.

Contrary to what you might think, you should put on *your* mask first. Not because you are selfish. Certainly not because you don't love your child. It is a simple matter of logistics. If you put your own mask on, you will have the oxygen you need to get your child's mask on. However, if you attempt to put your child's mask on first, you may pass out from lack of oxygen, and one or both of you may not make it. There's nothing selfish about taking care of yourself. It is the necessary prerequisite to taking care of others.

It is difficult to look need in the face and then walk away. But sometimes we are called to do that. We simply cannot do it all. God can, but we can't. So when we see needs that we cannot meet, let them motivate us to do the one thing that will make a difference: multiply ourselves by creating other disciples who may be called to meet those needs.

I pray that the opposite never happens, that you feel overwhelmed by these needs and simply give up trying, that you eventually become bored with your calling because there is so little you can do. Nothing is more likely to produce boring disciples than a bored teacher. Live with passion.

Go! Make disciples of all nations. Start with yourself. Start with your group. Become a committed disciple of Jesus, and then lead the people in your group to become disciples as well. We can reach the entire world for Christ through people like you.